SOLUTIONS FOCUS WORKING

Advance praise for Solutions Focus Working . . .

"There's a big difference between simplistic and simple. The former tends to be superficial (largely because it's on the "near side of complexity") while the latter is profound (having arrived on the "far side of complexity"). Mark McKergow and Jenny Clarke have delivered the latter – a very informative book filled with the wisdom of profound simplicity. I highly recommend this insightful and practical book."

Stephen M. R. Covey, author of The Speed of Trust

"A superb book for anyone interested in how to address change, clearly laid out and with a range of different types of interventions and organisations. The case studies highlight the benefits to real managers in real organisations facing real issues! There will definitely be something for you in this book whether you are a manager, a coach, a change agent or simply someone who wants to understand how the SF approach can work in organisations. This extremely well laid out and practical book brings together both the theory and practice of the SF approach to change in a crystal clear way."

Mike Brent, Programme Director, Ashridge Business School

"This book shows a number of paradoxes at play. To go faster, go slower. To achieve a vision, don't develop a concrete strategy. To achieve great change, take small steps. To get it right, tell people when you've got it wrong – and do something different. Applying the SIMPLE approach is not always easy. Thankfully, as these real-world case studies show, it is clear that it can be energising, engaging – and enjoyable! The SF approach is quick and fun, yet deep enough to deliver long-term lasting results."

Dr Emma Langman, Business Excellence Manager, Atkins

"The book is an invaluable practical resource book for people who are serious about developing people and creating real solutions. This is a practical guide from practitioners for practiners. It provides many examples and evidence that demonstrate that what works in real life does not need to be complicated."

Dr Sabine Dembkowski, Director, The Coaching Centre

Solutions Focus Working

Solutions Focus Working

80 real life lessons for successful organisational change

Mark McKergow and Jenny Clarke

Solutions Focus at Work Series

solutions
books

First published in Great Britain in 2007 by
SolutionsBooks
26 Christchurch Road
Cheltenham
GL50 2PL
United Kingdom
www.solutionsbooks.com

ISBN 978-0-9549749-4-7

Cover design by
Cathi Stevenson

Design, typesetting and production by
Action Publishing Technology Ltd

Contents

Acknowledgements

This book would not have been possible without the work and cooperation of the chapter co-authors and the organisations concerned. Our grateful thanks go to all those mentioned in the text. We also thank those contributors whose cases do not appear in the book for one reason or another – Alan Kay, Hans-Peter Korn and Veronika Kotrba.

We would like to thank our teachers and mentors, particularly Steve de Shazer and Insoo Kim Berg, co-founders of solution focused brief therapy who both died while this book was in preparation. We thank Michael Hjerth, Gale Miller, Matthias Varga von Kibéd and our Bristol Solutions Group colleagues.

Thanks to our many friends and colleagues in the SOLWorld community, who have organised and contributed to conferences, summer university events and the SOLUTIONS-L listserv discussion group. Thanks also to our own clients who have been the (sometimes unwitting) testbed for our ideas.

Wearing different hats, we gratefully acknowledge the skill and patience of Miles Bailey, Fiona Thornton and the team at Action Publishing Technology for making the publishing task so much easier.

Mark McKergow and Jenny Clarke
Cheltenham, March 2007

Chapter 1

Introducing Solutions Focus

'Change is happening all the time. The simple way to change is to find useful change and amplify it.'

This book is a massive fund of experience and know-how about keeping organisational change simple. The fourteen real life cases described here illustrate the Solutions Focus approach in action in a wide variety of situations, from widescale change to everyday effective management. Each case contains the viewpoints of those involved, and is rich in detail and perspective.

From these fourteen cases, we have drawn eighty lessons. These are by no means the only lessons in the book. They do, however, seem to be interesting to those wishing to use the Solutions Focus approach, either as leaders of change within organisations or as consultants and coaches.

The range of organisations who have worked with us in collecting this material is enormous. You will find cases relating to very large international organisations, including Lufthansa and Bayer CropScience. Other organisations are important within a national context, like the Cooperative Group, British Sky Broadcasting, the Ontario Medical Association and the Swedish employment service. Still others are much smaller, like the Maggazin sportswear chain from Austria or the EB Zurich educational institute in Switzerland. There are organisations from many sectors, including manufacturing (Freescale Semiconductor), financial services (Chelsea Building Society) and housing (Peabody Trust).

This collection also serves another purpose. Solutions Focus (SF) is a distinctive and minimal approach to change. From roots in therapy going back to the 1950s it has expanded into many fields including business and organisational change. Trying to define it in clear and unambiguous terms, however, is very challenging. The basic practice is so simple that it can look naïve and obvious. Closer examination reveals many differences from more traditional approaches, including mainstream OD, systems analysis and organisational psychology. Even practitioners of process consulting and Appreciative Inquiry will find some new ideas alongside well-established practices.

Simplicity in action

Solutions Focus derives from the therapeutic tradition of Solution Focused Brief Therapy (SFBT), founded by Steve de Shazer and Insoo Kim Berg from their Brief Family Therapy Center in Milwaukee. We discovered SFBT some fifteen years ago and were instantly struck by how relevant this approach could be for managers and consultants seeking to make progress in organisational settings. Since then the organisational world has started to discover and use SF ideas in many ways. There is now a thriving international community of practitioners who have gathered at the SOLWorld conferences and summer university events since 2002.

The three basic principles of SF are, in order of priority:

1. Don't fix what isn't broken
2. Find what works and do more of it
3. If it doesn't work, stop it and do something different

Don't fix what isn't broken is broadly a caution: be very clear about who wants what to be different. The fact that one person sees change as desirable is a start. However, if that person then starts to interfere with things that others think are not broken or in need of alteration, then things usually start to get difficult. So, engaging those involved around some kind of broadly agreed project is usually a good start.

Find what works and do more of it is the mainstay of the SF approach. In order to do this, we need some kind of guideline about the meaning of 'works'. This is based on what the people in this particular case want. The 'solution' in Solutions Focus is precisely this – what is wanted. This differs from the usual everyday meaning of the word solution; something to do, something to solve a problem. To be sure, you will discover how to make things better by using SF. However, this is not our use of the word 'solution'. Solutions Focus is therefore not a terribly good name for what we do – but it's the one we have.

What makes SF unusual is that rather than having found a

method and deciding that it works, we seek to start afresh in each case and find what works there. We also seek to keep the process as simple and clean as possible. There are some tools which are commonly used to get this process underway, which will be described below. As you read the various cases, bear in mind that in each case the people involved are engaged in a search for what works for them, in their particular context.

If it doesn't work, stop it and do something different is the emergency back-up principle. In most cases, simply finding what works and taking actions to build on that is sufficient. Occasionally, when nothing can be found that seems to help, it may be time to stop digging, get out of the hole and look for an alternative route. This principle can be applied to a stuck organisation – when nothing's working it's time to stand back and take stock. If you push on the Pull door, no progress will result. If you then push harder, still nothing. As soon as you stop and start to pull, however, there is a discernable change that lets you know that things are now moving.

This third principle is called into action infrequently – it appears only once in this book. It gets used only when a significant and persistent effort to find what works has proved less than successful. However, this is an important adjunct to the idea of finding what works, and is just as much a part of the SF methodology.

Keep things as simple as possible but no simpler – Albert Einstein

The three principles above are brought into action with a close eye on the idea of keeping things as simple as possible but no simpler. This quote by Albert Einstein is a modern statement of the philosophical principle called Occam's Razor. William of Occam was an English monk and writer from the 13th century. He studied philosophy at a time when the dominant Scholastic school was intent on devising ever-more-complicated theories to explain the world around them. Basically, more complicated ideas were cleverer, and therefore more advanced and better. William railed against this approach and wrote his famous principle:

'It is vain to do with more what can be done with fewer' – *William of Occam*

The simplest explanation, idea or theory that fits the facts and gets the desired results is to be preferred. Unnecessary concepts, properties and assumptions are to be cut away – as if with a razor. This idea is fundamental to philosophy and science to this day.

The idea that it is 'vain' to be more complicated than necessary works in two ways. Firstly, it is vain in the sense of being futile – there is no point in using more where less will achieve the same result. Secondly, it is vain in the sense of vanity – those who would have us believe that their more complicated ideas are superior may be doing so mistakenly to enhance their own reputations.

What are the grounds for thinking that the simple practice of SF is effective? Research into the approach in many fields (Macdonald, 2007) including therapy, education and now organisational work shows again and again that the SF approach delivers results as good or better than alternative methods, in less time.

The benefits of simplicity

Using Occam's Razor brings many practical benefits. It allows you to focus your attention and efforts clearly on the things which can start to make a difference. This in turn means less wasted effort, time and resource. The search for what works is usually a positive and energising process, as many of the cases in this book will testify. Being highly attuned to noticing what is working leads to a clean and respectful practice, which is experienced as empowering and helpful by those involved. Being less confused yourself helps to keep confusion amongst others to a minimum. And ultimately, you can start to see how many everyday concepts and practices can be simplified or overlooked.

Six SIMPLE principles

> 'The art of being wise is the art of knowing what to overlook' – William James

In their book The Solutions Focus, Mark and co-author Paul Z Jackson defined SF practice in terms not only of simplicity but also in six SIMPLE principles. These principles are a guide to how to stay simple, by knowing what to focus on and what, in the words of William James, to overlook. Bearing in mind the difficulties of trying to clearly define a field where definitions are treated sceptically, we present them here. These principles will prepare you for the nature of SF practice in the cases that follow. The principles are:

Solutions – not problems
Inbetween – not individual
Make use of what's there – not what isn't
Possibilities from past, present and future
Language – clear, not complicated
Every case is different – beware ill-fitting theory

Solutions – not problems

In a field calling itself Solutions Focus this may seem obvious. However, this principle is often misunderstood. The 'solution' here is not something to do next (though that will emerge) but what is wanted. This is made clear in our Albert Model (named after Albert Einstein and his famous quotation 'Things should be made as simple as possible, but no simpler').

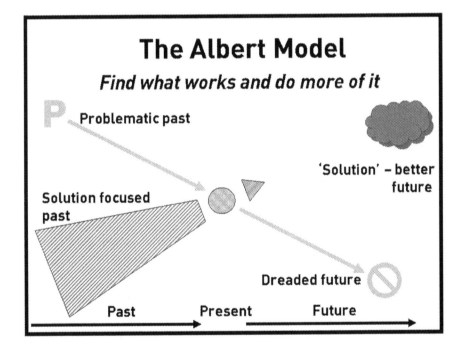

At the heart of the SF approach is this distinction between narratives relating to the problem – what's wrong – and the solution – what's wanted. Most approaches to change seek to discover what to do next by examining the problem and seeking to address it. This works well for broken motor cars and washing machines, but less well for people and organisations. The insight of SF is that these two narratives are not related. Take five people with the same 'problem', ask them about signs that things are improving and you get five different answers. There is much more relevant information in the details of what's wanted than in the story of what's wrong.

At the same time, there is a (sometimes thin and ignored) narrative of elements or enablers of the 'solution' which have happened in the past, and may well be continuing to happen in the present. SF practitioners start to connect up these elements and look for small steps to build on what is working. The small steps, often taken as some kind of experiment, start to move things forwards and give even more information about what helps in this case. Then what works can be used and built on with even more confidence and so on.

In the cases that follow you will find many examples and methods of this shift from looking at the problem axis to the solution axis. It can take skill and patience. However, the advantage of leaving the problem and its diagnosis behind are considerable, both in terms of motivation and time.

Inbetween – not individual

This is the most conceptual of the six SIMPLE principles. A key element of SF practice is the Interactional View, originally deriving from the work of Gregory Bateson's research project into communications which developed into family therapy and then brief therapy in the 1960s. Following the development of the simpler SFBT, Steve de Shazer drew connections with the philosophy of Ludwig Wittgenstein, whose later work forms a basis for post-structural linguistics. We are continuing to develop these connections today, including connections with discursive psychology and the science of emergence.

Conventional wisdom has it that individual behaviour is driven from within – by values, beliefs, motivations and many more. The 'inbetween' view is that trying to explain behaviour by reference to internal states is misleading. In practice people develop their faculties interacting with others, and so learn to speak and act during conversations. Even when they are thinking 'alone', they are doing so in the context of their prior interactional experience.

The practical upshot of this is to greatly enhance simplicity. Just don't use 'mentalistic' language about beliefs, values and so on. Instead, keep it simple by using interactional language relating to observable signs and activity. During the cases you will find many references to 'signs that things are better' or 'what would be the first sign your colleagues noticed'. These are examples of questions to prompt interactional language.

Why is this a good idea? Because the findings from research into the effectiveness of SF practice show results that are as good or better than other approaches, in less time. It therefore seems the case that such mentalistic language is not necessary to produce change. Indeed, it may be serving to muddle the issue and delay change. This is another example of the benefit of taking simplicity seriously.

Make use of what's there – not what isn't

SF is about finding what works in a particular given context. Therefore, anything that seems to be connected with things working, going better or even going less badly than normal may be worth utilising. This includes personal strengths, positive qualities, skills and co-operation as well as examples of the 'solution' happening already.

This may seem obvious. However, it's quite different to the commonly used idea of 'gap analysis', where the *differences* between the present and the desired future are the most important aspects. It's not unusual to find managers who quickly nod towards what's already going well before getting onto the allegedly more relevant topic of what is not. This is not to say that organisations should not be aware of these differences. It's simply that the building blocks for change are much more likely to come from what's already going well. You will find the practical application of this principle in every case in the book.

Possibilities from past, present and future

A sense of future possibility, of hope and optimism and positive expectations, is of course vital in any change effort. Where there is no hope, things are very difficult. The idea of possibilities in the past, however, is perhaps a more novel idea. Some think that the past has happened, is gone, is immutable. We take a different view. The past is a useful source of stories of success, examples of resources in action, even tales of adversity overcome.

The key to bringing these stories into the present, where they can influence the future, lies in identifying and drawing out their connections with the 'solution' – what's wanted. It is much easier in practice to identify relevant examples if you have some idea what you are looking for.

The idea of possibilities is also different from certainties. As soon as you become certain of what's going to happen, or indeed what happened in the past, it's much harder to start to identify the alternative possibilities. In some cases people use explanations of the past to create a firm (and unhelpful) view of the future. In SF practice we tend to steer away from explanations towards experiments and a sense of 'seeking to find what works' – particularly if the explanation is about why the problem happens and is difficult to change.

Language – clear, not complicated

One of the working principles of SF is the idea that '$5 words may be worth more than $5000 words'. $5000 words are usually long, complicated and abstract, and sound very impressive. They are often used in explanation, theorising and academia. $5 words, on the other hand, are short, concrete and detailed. They may not sound very impressive. They are, however, usually more connected to action, movement and everyday life.

In the cases described here, you will find many examples of people gently seeking to simplify the language being used. The focus will be on the language used by the people involved in going about their everyday business, rather than on abstract and generalising language imposed by observers. This turns out to be a surprisingly practical idea – it not only shows respect to those involved by taking their words seriously, it is also a good way to avoid getting into dubious explanations and generalisations.

Every case is different – avoid ill-fitting theory

Most approaches to organisational change seek to simplify the messy everyday world by establishing some classification scheme. If the issue is of type X, then action A is advised. This is also true of science, medicine and many other fields, and has served humanity very well.

SF works in a different way. Simply approach each case with a completely clean and open mind, seek to identify what the people want and what works. If you 'know' what should work, then you will undoubtedly try to find it and will therefore miss important clues. Not knowing what should be done is the easiest way to see clearly. In the words of Zen writer Shunryu Suzuki, 'In the mind of the expert, there are few possibilities. In the mind of the beginner there are many.' So it may be more helpful to have the mind of the beginner than the mind of the expert.

Of course there are many occasions when theories may be helpful. In these cases, we urge people to go on using them. When preconceived ideas are failing to fit your experience, however, you may find it helpful to let go of the idea and examine your experience again with fresh eyes.

In the cases described here you will find little in the way of conventional models and theories of organisation. This is not because we don't know these models. It is because we are exploring a different, and ostensibly more effective, way to work.

Solutions Tools

As you can see from the ideas outlined above, there are many possible ways to use SF ideas in practice. Over the years a number of practical tools have emerged. Some of these tools are mentioned in the case descriptions.

In The Solutions Focus book, Mark and Paul outlined six of these tools as the basics of the SF toolkit. They have passed into common usage in the field, and are useful ways to delineate some of the practical activities.

You begin with the **Platform** – which may be derived from the problem. This is a point of departure for the process of searching for what works. Key parts of the Platform are identifying the customers for change – people who both want something to be different and are prepared to do something about it – and getting a general sense of what's wanted.

A leap of the imagination can launch you from the platform directly to the **Future Perfect** – a description of everyday life with the problem vanished, the way the customers for change want it to be. This is sometimes prompted by asking the Miracle Question; suppose there was a miracle tonight and the problem disappeared – what would be the signs tomorrow that would let you know that the miracle had happened?

A **Scale** may help in connecting what's wanted with what's working. In SF practice scales are typically from 0–10, and can be very helpful in identifying differences that make a difference and establishing progress.

Next you might accumulate **Counters** – what's working already, resources, skills, know-how and expertise that will count in getting you towards the solution. The word counter relates to something that counts (ie something that matters), is counter to the problem (ie is connected to the solution) and is good to pile up and collect.

The **Affirm** tool relates to identifying, naming and discussing the useful strengths and qualities brought by those involved.

Rather than build up a long term action plan, SF practice is more concerned with choosing **Small Actions** that the participants take to help move forward. It is often astonishing how small a well-chosen action can be and still make a big difference.

Naturally, you note any differences that the actions make, which adds to the pile of counters. Any progress is a further counter towards a solution, and allows a fresh visit into further affirmations and choices of the next small steps.

It is quite possible to find different ways of doing SF which do not involve using these tools in this way. New tools are being devised and different people may describe their practice differently.

Defining SF – a quandary

In his classic work Philosophical Investigations, Ludwig Wittgenstein faced a dilemma. As his endeavour was to show the futility of constructing general theories and explanations as a way to make philosophical progress, Wittgenstein correctly realised that to state this as a general theory would be self-defeating and contrary. Rather than describe what he was *not* advocating, he set out to convey his ideas of a new way of inquiry by showing example after example.

SF can be seen as a way of inquiry in the same post-structural tradition as Wittgenstein. We therefore face a similar problem: how to describe a rigorous and well-proven methodology which has a central idea that every case is different, without appearing to rule in or rule out actions which may prove highly fruitful in one case and utterly perverse in another.

This collection, therefore, can be taken as multiplicity of descriptions of SF in action in organisational settings. Having read through it, you will have a much greater understanding of the different ways in which the SF approach can appear and be useful in the most challenging contexts in the workplace.

Recognising this contradiction, however, we have attempted to summarise some aspects of SF practice. You may find this helpful in attuning your eyes and ears before reading the cases. You may also find that it serves to answer some questions about the many aspects of consulting, coaching and change which do not appear within these pages. Like Wittgenstein, we do not intend to take time talking about the things we do not do. In this introduction, however, we hope we have shown that the SF approach is comprehensive in its own simple way, and that the alternative approaches which might have been used have been overlooked intentionally rather than simply forgotten.

How to use this book

There is a great variety of material and slants to SF practice described here. You might want to identify a case that looks interesting and start from there. Alternatively you could go to the eighty lessons listed at the book of the book, find one that appeals and then read about how it appeared in practice. You could start at the beginning – we have chosen to start with cases showing some of the basic ideas of SF practice. Or you could just open the book and dip in.

Whatever you do, we urge you to use this book to inspire your own work. The cases here are not recipes for success, they are signposts to future possibilities.

References
Paul Z Jackson and Mark McKergow (2007), The Solutions Focus: Making Coaching and Change SIMPLE, London: Nicholas Brealey Publishing (2nd revised edition)

Alasdair Macdonald (2007), Solution-focused Therapy: Theory, Research and Practice, London: Sage Publications

Ludwig Wittgenstein (1958), Philosophical Investigations (tr. GEM Anscombe), Oxford: Blackwell

Chapter 2

The power of one

When coaching one man changes an organisation

Co-author: Carey Glass

Organisation: Cooperative Group

After a big restructuring, morale was low across the whole organisation. How could one person start to turn things around, taking actions so small that many went un-noticed, and with the help of just four sessions of SF coaching ...

Sometimes you can be lucky. You can hit upon the difference that is going to make the biggest difference in an organisation quickly. That is what happened with Paul Carpenter.

Paul's boss ran a one-billion pound conglomerate inside the Cooperative Group, one of the UK's largest mutual organisations. She offered Paul, who came from an engineering background and ran its building services and facilities management business, the opportunity for some one-to-one leadership coaching. Having experienced some Solution Focused work herself, she thought Solutions Focus might have something to offer him and introduced him to Carey Glass.

They chatted on the phone; it became apparent that the brief was to coach one man to change the morale and motivation of the entire business following a pervasive restructure. What a fascinating possibility. Would it be achievable? What would it say about how you can go about change in organisations? Could it be achieved without grand and expensive change schemes – the business had 500 employees and a 50 million pound turnover? Could SF work in this way?

Paul was sceptical of coaching. He later said:

'My background had been very much in engineering, manufacturing, traditionally male-dominated industries where any kind of assistance with leadership was looked upon as a bit soft and a bit flowery. The attitude was 'What do you need this for, just get on with it.' So I was a little bit, or a lot sceptical at first but I was also intrigued ... .'

Yet Paul became the difference that made the biggest difference in the organisation. He had various qualities that allowed change to be made easily and quickly. He listened openly and genuinely when he and Carey met. He was willing to try things in the business. He could see things simply. He did not complicate matters to prevent action. He was not a nay-sayer. And most importantly, he did not let his ego interfere with his actions. He tried stuff. If it worked he continued it. If it didn't he accepted it and moved on.

To Carey's surprise, they only used 4 afternoon meetings to effect the change in morale and motivation. What follows is the story of how they did it.

Paint the picture and paint it clearly

One of the things you learn about Solutions Focus is to trust the process. So Paul spent the first four hour session answering the following basic SF questions for each team in head office: reception, finance, customer services and the engineering team made up of contract managers, engineers and estimators. The first question was

How would you know that there is no longer a morale problem in this group?

This question asks someone to describe what the world would look like if their problem was gone. You can replace the word 'morale' with whatever problem you are facing and it works swimmingly. People usually think about the problem, rather than imagining what life would look like if it was absent. Actually imagining what it would look like by asking this question can be crucial to moving forward (de Shazer 1978a).

It is important to paint that picture clearly. You need to describe that world in detail, as if you were watching it on a video. How would you be spending your time? What would you be saying or doing? What would others be saying or doing? Painting the picture in detail means describing what you and others would be saying or doing on a daily basis. This is usefully called describing the preferred future (George, Iveson and Ratner, 1990) or the Future Perfect (Jackson and McKergow, 2002).

Change programs often miss a critical point. They describe the goals or change strategy, but they describe them in the abstract or in chunks that are too large to be useful. Ultimately change only happens on the basis of what we choose to say and do everyday. If we don't say and do things differently on a daily basis, change doesn't happen. So we need to describe change at that behavioural level so that it's easy to make it happen.

What happens when people answer this sort of SF question is that it becomes a liberating experience for them and this is reflected on their faces. Possibilities are unleashed, imaginations run free, they can start to see what to do and feel relieved. The key when painting the picture is to encourage people to make their answers small and detailed enough so that it becomes obvious to them that they can act.

Build a picture of unconstrained detail

This combination of an unconstrained description of a better future and tiny specific details is a key element of the Solutions Focus approach. The smallness of the detail seems to help in a number of ways: motivation towards a compelling possibility, concrete details which could be easily spotted and clarity about the possibility of moving forwards.

Here is a small extract of what Paul described for the engineering group:

- *They will encourage people along side them.*
- *I would feel more welcoming to people and I would know everyone's names.*
- *Their manager would make them aware of the strength of the order book and their position in the market.*
- *They would be generating work and ideas up the line.*
- *You would see a handful of people giving off the aura of wanting to further their careers and be ready for promotion.*
- *The posture of people would be different – it would show they were happy to be at work.*
- *People at desks would be clearly working on a particular task*

Once described this way, Paul could easily pick out things to start doing.

For a start, he decided to move a strong team player into the engineering group who was good at encouraging people alongside her, to help them encourage each other.

As well, he realised that his perceptions of this group could be affected by the fact that he didn't know them very well. After work one evening he wandered up to the 6th floor where they were located and looked at their desks and pin boards to find things in common to talk about so that he could get to know them better and did so. In an ensuing discussion about golf, they started to offer ideas up the line. Three of the engineering team offered to set up a golf tournament as a marketing exercise for the group's clients. Forty five clients attended what became an excellent business development opportunity. On getting to know the engineers, Paul changed his perception. He realised that they had more energy than he thought, were working hard on particular tasks, but were simply more reserved in style.

The company had gone through a restructure that had led up to an 80% change in staff in some departments. Just as Paul didn't know everyone, he also realised that this may be a common problem. So he asked one of the staff to draw up floor plans to be pinned up with everyone's names on them so that people could subtly learn each other's names. In these ways he started to take small actions that would lead to the preferred future that he had described.

Define Strengths

Paul answered two more questions about each team in the first meeting:

Where is each team on a scale of 0–10 in terms of morale?

How come they are already at that number and what did they do to contribute to success last year?

The first question provides a scale for measuring where you are at and noticing changes. Scales give perspective by allowing people to stand outside their actions and notice what they have achieved and what they may still like to do.

This second question turns the usual approach to problem-solving on its head. Normally, especially with a low score, one might ask 'Why are we only 2 or 4?' which leads to a deeper analysis of our problems. The question 'why are we already at 2 or 4 or 7 on the scale?' is much more useful. You can spend a lot of time analysing weaknesses through the 'why are we only' type of questions, and even when you can answer them, the answer doesn't necessarily tell you what to do about them. 'Why are we already' questions point to what is working, and what strengths are helping towards our ultimate goal. You will notice what a refreshing difference asking the question this way made for Paul.

He decided that the engineers were at 4. Here is an extract of what they had contributed to bring them to 4:

- *They had undergone a period of really difficult change and had come out the other end!*
- *Three members of the team had built up good relations with another company whom they were partnering on 30–40% of work.*
- *Clients were talking about their quality and dedication.*
- *They had won a large number of smaller contracts and widened the client base.*

In that discussion Paul also said:

'They only tend to hear the bad feedback and their own self-perception is that they are not at the forefront of the market place. Because the business has not entirely turned around yet, no one's valuing the achievements along the way.'

Thinking about what was already working refreshed Paul's view of the strengths of his team and made it so much easier to produce more actions to add to his 'to do list' such as:

- *Encourage their manager to give the team feedback on each step of positive progress.*
- *Keep them informed of their position in the market.*
- *Begin the Christmas function by highlighting last year's achievement in each team.*
- *Send out good news bulletins whenever there was some good news to tell.*
- *Institute a half yearly road show to mark achievements.*
- *Involve more staff in monthly regional meetings.*

In contrast to the usual SWOT analysis, a Solutions Focused

approach would suggest dispensing with the weaknesses section as it is not considered very useful in working towards solutions. Indeed there is significant evidence coming from the discipline of psychology that a positive approach liberates our thinking and creativity to move forward.

Never mind the weaknesses . . .

It may well be that the very idea of investing time in fixing weaknesses, as opposed to developing strengths, is flawed. In some organisations we still come across the idea that people have two things – strengths (which are welcome) and 'areas for development' (also known as weaknesses – to be worked on). How might it be if the strengths *were* the areas for development?

Use comparisons to move you forward rather than bring you down

By asking questions about each team Paul and Carey had produced a baseline for morale and motivation across the organisation. The advantage of this was that they could compare areas. However, it is the Solution Focused way in which areas are compared that is essential to improving morale and performance rather than creating a decline. Paul could see that morale was lower on the 6th floor than the 1st floor, so Carey posed the questions:

'What makes morale better on the first floor than on the sixth floor?'

followed by:

'What have we discovered that is working on the first floor that we can transfer to the sixth floor?'

Problem-focused thinking would usually lead you to ask the question this way: 'Why is morale worse on the 6th floor?'. This tends to extend the list of problems to be solved and doesn't generate solutions. Solution Focused thinkers recognise that it is more productive to ask about what is working well in one place, because once you have stated those answers you may be able to transfer some of those solutions to the area needing support. As well, positive questions free people to come up with ideas. As you will notice, using comparisons positively, made it easy for Paul to see what to do.

Paul answered:

> *'The first floor is very much management and finance, whereas the sixth floor is clerical, administration and engineering and although I try and get up there once a day, I probably only spend five or ten minutes. I have greater interaction with the people on my floor, they probably feel more in the know and more involved in the business.'*

By analysing what was working on the first floor, Paul took the following actions.

He moved two senior managers to work in the middle of the clerical and administrative teams on the sixth floor so that they would feel less isolated from management.

> *'As a result people felt more involved. They liked being the right hand for the senior management people on the floor, they felt there was more going on in the company, sensed more leadership and started to bring ideas to these two managers of how things could be improved. Out of this several deputies emerged who were soon promoted.'*

He started a glossy employee newsletter that went out nationally to keep people informed about the business. As well, 'Let's Do It Better' focus groups were started around the country to operate as ideas forums. While there was scepticism at first, more and more people started to attend them.

Had Paul analysed why morale was worse on the 6th floor he may never have got to these ideas. Even if he had come up with the idea of moving managers to the 6th floor by asking what is worse about the 6th floor, it is important to be aware that the way we ask questions reflects and informs our attitude. When we ask problem-focused questions our ideas can carry a problem-focused attitude along with them. In that light, moving the managers may have been perceived by the 6th floor as checking up on them rather than welcoming them.

As a result of these questions, Paul had put 12 different actions into place during the two months between the first and second meetings, and 6 more were being actively planned.

> ### *Invisible actions can lead to visible change*
>
> This case is very notable for the sheer number of small actions set rolling by Paul during the project. We will discover later on how many of them had a positive effect, and how few of them were seen as 'change initiatives' by the staff.

Scaling on the Floor

At the end of the work Paul and Carey spent some time reflecting on what aspects of Solution Focused coaching assisted him in working out what to do. One of the techniques he found most helpful was actually standing on a scale of numbers that had been placed on the floor composed of 11 pieces of card numbered 0 – 10.

Paul found that experiencing the scale by standing and moving around on it was much more powerful than looking at a scale on a piece of paper. Somehow he couldn't keep it at a distance when he was walking on it. Becoming an actor in the process focused Paul's mind. He also liked the fact that the scale was not a continuous line. Using separate cards made Paul think about the scale as a series of steps. His attention was drawn to each gap, one by one, and he focused on the actions he could take to bridge it as he moved up the steps towards his goal.

Scales are a Solutions Focused technique (de Shazer 1994) that can be applied in all sorts of ways. You might like to try using them with this exercise.

Don't look for the causes of problems

At the second coaching session Paul explained that one of the issues that was contributing to low morale was that the staff were separated on two floors with five levels between them. That wasn't conducive to just nipping up and down stairs to see each other. He was dependent on another organisation moving out in order to have everyone on the same floor. He thought that morale would further improve once those on the 6th floor could move to the space vacated by the other organisation. In the meantime they would just have to wait.

Feeling a bit stuck in this situation, Carey asked what Paul would do after the move.

'Once they've moved I'd like to get people together on a social event to make sure they interact. Also a lot of new people have joined the company and I think I'd have an overall induction because they might not be sure quite how their roles contribute to the organisation.'

They wondered what would happen if Paul did those things now:

'I naturally thought I'd wait till people moved down and then we'd do it, but I suppose there's no reason why we can't get that moving now and it might in fact help the overall move between the two floors and help people gel better.'

He instituted the social events and a few months later he noticed that there was a lot more movement between the two floors.

From this discussion Paul also decided that when the 6th floor did move, rather than bolt people on to the current teams by putting them in the vacated space, he would move everyone around and get them interacting that way as well.

We have been educated to believe that if we ask ourselves 'why' in order to find the cause of a problem, we can work out what to do about it. However this story highlights a premise of Solution Focused thinking that looking for the cause of a problem, doesn't necessarily lead you to useful outcomes. Rather, looking for a cause may well exacerbate the problem and leave you feeling stuck. It was natural to assume, having found that teams on different floors was a cause of the morale problem, that reversing it would solve the problem and so the organisation would wait till that could happen. Actually, just waiting was exacerbating a sense of separation, and preventing a search for alternatives. As well, while moving floors would have helped, that act alone would not have instantly solved the sense of separation that staff were experiencing without further action to enable the group to realign as one team. So asking people to imagine what would happen beyond the point at which they are stuck often releases them to find new options. Thinking about what would happen after the move enabled Paul to see activities that could be implemented immediately to decrease the isolation and improve morale even with staff on separate floors. He was no longer stuck waiting to act. Solutions Focused thinkers argue that it's better not to look for causes (de Shazer 1988). But if you are getting stuck having found them, imagine life when they are no longer a problem in order to move forward.

Find what caused the progress, not what caused the problem

For people who enjoy causal analysis, there is another way to use causes while maintaining an SF approach. Look for the causes of the 'solution' rather than the problem. This can be particularly effective if the causes give an opportunity for sharing of credit amongst those who were involved in making the cause happen.

Take an experimental attitude

By the end of January, Paul had instigated 20 or more new actions to improve morale. In the following meetings Carey and Paul tracked what was and wasn't working and added some more actions. Carey says:

> 'One of Paul's great qualities was his willingness to try things and care about them but not invest his own ego in their success. He could stand back from circumstances, and take a measured look at whether his efforts were bearing fruit and change course as required. Observing Paul made me realise the importance of having an experimental attitude when implementing change programmes.'

Solutions Focus offers a different approach to organisational strategy. Akin to most organisational change programs the approach establishes a vision, although with a greater use of the imagination than many models would incorporate. However it doesn't set a long-term strategy to get to the vision, or at most it sets it in mud rather than stone. People working in Solutions Focused ways are on the look out to find what works and do more of it and to stop doing what doesn't work and do something different (de Shazer 1985). So, in order to get to the vision, they need to try things, see if they work, and change course if they don't. That's about as strategic as it gets. It's easier to change course if you take it step by step and if your strategy is set in mud rather than in stone. And it also takes a certain amount of maturity to try things and drop them. It's common to find organisations and political bodies that wed themselves to their strategy rather than observing how it's working in reality. Sometimes it's the belief in the strategy that gets in the way, sometimes it's the ego. But Paul had none of these problems.

Stop doing what doesn't work and do something different

In one of the conversations Paul started to discuss one of the managers who had been promoted. Nick was the best salesman in the company. He had grown sales year on year and was also good at managing his own operations team. On the back of those strengths he had been promoted to general management, controlling the business operation in the area in which he had previously controlled sales. While his sales performance was still strong, Nick did not enjoy the rigours of administration and finance and performance in these areas under his management needed improvement. Despite the promotion and support to improve his performance, Nick was not as happy as he had been in his previous role. And Paul was spending significant amounts of his own time on these issues.

It is both bizarre and common in organisations that we hire employees for their strengths and spend our time and performance management focusing on their weaknesses. Managers commonly spend significant amount of their time on poor performance, some of which surely emanates from this incoherency.

A Solutions Focused approach aims to find what works and do more of it. In this situation the organisation had found what worked, Nick's sale skills, and limited them.

Paul could see that he had to stop doing what wasn't working; it was not good for Nick or the organisation. He recognised that he should work to Nick's strengths as well as the strengths of others in the business. He added an experienced team with an administration manager reporting to Nick and enabled him, still as a general manager, to have the leeway to get on with what he was good at. Sales increased as a result, the management of administration and finance improved, and Paul's time was released for other ends. He recognised what worked for individuals and created circumstances to enable them to flourish. Since then, Nick has been promoted to Managing Director of the division.

> ### Stop doing what doesn't work and do something different
>
> Paul was wise here to apply the principles of 'Stop doing what doesn't work and do something different'. This principle is a part of the SF approach and yet is rarely applied – the simpler principle of 'find what works and do more of it' is usually sufficient. However, on occasions when the very direct route seems to produce no progress it can be useful to experiment with a little 'do something different'.

Over time Paul could see that following some of the positive changes he had made to provide information and foster involvement, there was now a thirst for more information and more involvement. He thought it would be tremendous for morale if employees knew even more about what they'd achieved and where they were going. After all, the customer services department had been answering more calls, the success rate of tenders made to suppliers had improved, the speed of payments made to suppliers had improved as had the debt recovery rate. So Paul arranged for performance indicator graphs to be put up in the relevant departments to demonstrate these achievements. He and Carey were sure that providing this objective evidence would further boost morale.

At the end of the sessions, Carey collected a group of staff together to obtain their perspective on morale in the organisation. She took them through the changes that had been instituted and asked how each one had affected morale. She discovered that the performance indicator graphs had had no impact on morale at all. Indeed, by the time they had filtered down onto the walls of the organisation, the staff thought they were there as management information rather than as a proud record of their personal success.

The same applied to the floor plans with names on them that had been pinned up. Staff felt that the lack of introductions during the restructure had been bad for morale. However the floor plans had been produced too late as staff had met those they needed to know for work. Knowing the names of the others didn't expand their interactions as hoped. Carey recalls:

'Paul's experimental attitude towards change really assisted when receiving feedback from staff. With this feedback, he simply accepted that

it was time to stop doing what wasn't working and do something different.'

Notice what is emerging

Paul and Carey found assistance here by noticing what had emerged that had nothing to do with their plans. In the feedback session one person commented that she and another individual, rather than using the performance graphs, had started to talk to the engineers about management information, and that they loved it. They were providing the engineers with information about client feedback that had come through the customer support centre and were discussing performance against targets. The engineers loved it so much that they kept asking for more and started to use it to create competition amongst themselves to bring in more business. Carey says:

'Paul recognised the importance of what had emerged and encouraged and expanded the sharing of management information by tailoring it to suit different needs in the business. He wasn't embarrassed about the things that didn't work, and was wise enough to move on and notice the things that did.'

These are examples of why taking an experimental attitude is so important in moving an organisation forward. In reality, because organisations embody the complexity and intricacy of human inter-actions, none of us can accurately predict what impact our interventions will have. Therefore the more possibilities for action, the better our chances of finding the ones that are helpful. An exper-imental attitude allows us to try some, keep the ones that work, discard the ones that don't and then try some others. It also allows us to notice what is emerging that we didn't expect so we can move forward. In organisations we are masterful at noticing what is emerging that we didn't expect; but we usually notice the things that are wrong and that we don't like. What would happen if we used that mastery to start noticing and capitalising on what is emerging and working?

Change is happening all the time – just look for the useful change

Change is happening all the time. At least, that's a useful presupposition to start with. And if change is happening all the time, then perhaps it's a good idea to be very aware of useful change that's happening, even if we didn't start it, seek it or even expect it. Framing actions as small experiments is a very good way to prepare ourselves to watch carefully for the results, and build on the most useful ones. After all, if we plant ten seeds and eight of them sprout, our first concern is not with the other two.

Find what works and do more of it

One day Paul went to visit one of the largest and long established clients of the business whose contract renewal valued in the millions was coming up. He went in to tell them of all the good things that were happening in the business, but before he could, they sat him down to discuss a plethora of concerns that would prevent this pivotal contract being renewed. While the work on site was very good, the invoicing, contract management and administration were poor. Paul returned to work and set up a project team to address each issue systematically for this client. He selectively brought in consultants and with training and additional staff they managed to resolve the contracting issues. However, they couldn't resolve the invoicing which had been problematic for two years. Despite their best efforts the same problems would recur. Having inculcated Solutions Focused thinking Paul finally decided to get the team together himself and take a Solutions Focused approach to the issue. He said to the team:

> 'We keep focusing too much on the problem with this issue. Is there another client with similar work, where we use a different method of invoicing that works? Could we take that model and put it in place for this client?'

After a bit of 'umming and aaahing' and adapting the model to the client's needs, this was done. The client, somewhat sceptical, insisted on seeing whether it would work for a few months before even considering renegotiations. The Solution Focused approach of finding what worked and doing more of it, bore fruit. Soon after, a multi-million dollar contract was signed for a further three years.

What worked elsewhere?

This is a nice example of finding what works elsewhere, and seeing what of that know-how can be brought into the problematic situation. The objective is to find ideas that will fit the present context. This is most easily done by looking directly into the present context – when do things go better? However, seeking inspiration from other sources can be valuable too – as long as the ideas discovered are allowed to flex and fit into the situation at hand.

The results

Paul and Carey first met in November followed by sessions in January, March and May. In August Carey met with a random selection of staff to get their impressions of the changes since the restructure and their ratings of morale in the business. Thirty-five different small actions to improve morale had either been put into place or emerged over those months and she was curious to find out from the staff's perspective whether morale had improved, and if so, which actions they thought had contributed to the improvement.

They told the story of the restructure and on a scale of 1 to 10 rated morale at various points in this history: before the restructure, during it and at the point at which they met. The results are shown in the graph below. The staff were clear that morale had improved and rated it at 7.5 when business conditions were strong.

Of the various actions that were taken to improve morale they felt that 26 had made a positive impact, 2 a negative impact and that there were 7 which either made no impact, hadn't been acted on or of which they were unaware.

Some of the 26 factors that they included were the half yearly roadshows, the monthly meetings in each region, more business information being passed to staff weekly including information about accounts, the new newsletter, social events, winning more business. Interestingly, of the 26 positive actions, 8 were emergent and unplanned. These included people wanting to know expectations, the introduction of uniforms in the customer services team, the advent of interstream competition, moving offices, and a decrease in staff turnover that was heartening. Carey remarks:

> *'What was really interesting was that the staff were unaware that there had been a determined effort to work on morale. However, they were very clear that things had improved dramatically.'*

Changes In Morale

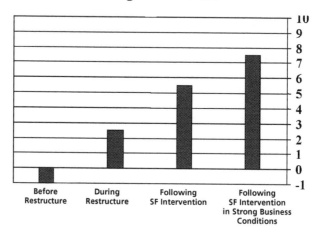

Effect of All Actions Taken To Improve Morale

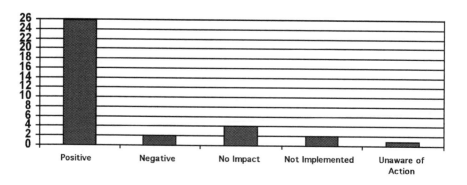

Small changes can be irresistible

These findings are a real testament to the gentle power of Solutions Focus. Change initiatives which are shouted from the rooftops can often result in wariness and resistance. When change is done guerrilla-style, as in this example, with small actions which seem part of the normal rhythm of work, there is nothing to resist. Change grows in an irresistible way.

The power of small steps

When you think about it, thirty or so actions is a lot of activity in a small amount of time for which you might assume Paul would have had to really gather together his energies. However Paul described it like this:

> 'These were just small initiatives, but each of them on the back of the others helped to continue to raise morale. Going away from each meeting with small actions to kick off the next day made it easy to start things moving with colleagues – this had a good impact on actually getting them done.'

What was critical in this achievement was the recognition that ultimately change occurs as a result of our everyday actions. This encapsulates one of the powerful advantages of a Solutions Focused approach. At the beginning of the process Carey had asked herself whether it was really possible to coach one man to change the morale and motivation of an entire organisation. Could it be achieved without grand and expensive change schemes? What became clearly apparent is that if a leader focuses on finding and doing what works in the everyday world, it can be achieved. The results of this realisation are manifold. For example, it might explain why technologically led change has often been successful because it quickly filters into our everyday actions. It also explains why other types of change programmes often don't work when high-level goals remain poorly translated or poorly communicated into everyday life. People require a description of what the goal means for their actions. This may not seem particularly lofty but painting the picture in everyday detail allows people to relate to and embrace change more easily and so that is the level at which the work needs to be done. It also means that change can be built up, small step after small step, success being assessed and everyday actions modified as required in order to get to the ultimate vision.

As a result Carey discovered that not only was it possible to change the morale of the organisation through one man, it was possible without consuming all of the organisation's time, teams, resources, energy and most importantly without consuming its goodwill. Carey sums up her experience in this case:

> 'Change works best when nobody notices it. When it happens inside the everyday activities of the business with small steps – so small that even

if they don't work there is no great disaster – they don't distract from the day to day business by focusing energy on change. It is when you start making a big deal of change that you get into the arguments. When you do it quietly, then it just happens and life improves.'

Paul has now moved on to a new business with new challenges within the Cooperative Group. Reflecting on the process, he says:

'It has equipped me far better to take on larger general management roles, and given me another set of tools to approach problems with business performance. The role I am now in is Number 2 in a larger company, with even greater challenges, but I feel equipped to improve the morale and improve business.'

References

Steve de Shazer. (1978a) Brief hypnotherapy of two sexual dysfunctions: The crystal ball technique. *American Journal of Clinical Hypnosis, 20(3),* 203–208

Steve de Shazer, (1985) *Keys to solution in brief therapy.* New York: Norton.

Steve de Shazer, (1988) *Clues: Investigating solutions in brief therapy,* New York: Norton.

Steve de Shazer, (1994) *Words Were Originally Magic.* New York: Norton

Evan George, Chris Iveson and Harvey Ratner, (1990) *Problem to Solution: Brief therapy with individuals and families.* London BT Press

Paul Z Jackson and Mark McKergow (2002) The Solutions Focus, London: Nicholas Brealey Publishing

Acknowledgement: The name of this case study has been inspired by Bryce Courtenay's book 'The Power of One'.

Carey Glass, Business Psychologist and Director of The Human Centre, works with leaders who want to shine from the UK's largest private sector and public service organisations, to foster success in their teams. An Aussie, who herself managed massive change as Director of Planning and Development of one of Adelaide's largest health service organisations, Carey now loves seeing the magic that occurs as she helps Chairs, Managers and teams transform UK organisations into communities of action and achievement.

Carey Glass, The Human Centre, 13 Street Lane, Leeds LS8 1BW
+44 (0)113 226 2738
thehumancentre@onetel.com

Chapter 3

Engaging people for innovation

Bringing strategy to life in Canadian healthcare

Co-author: Minna Graham

Organisation: Professional Service Department of the Ontario Medical Association

Change is in the air ... opportunities beckon ... but how to engage an entire department to work with, support and build on a corporate strategy? In this chapter Canadian facilitator Minna Graham uses Solutions Focus in a neat and well-executed way to help some top health professionals find ways to go on together.

The Ontario Medical Association (OMA) is a voluntary association founded in 1880 to represent the political, clinical and economic interests of the province's medical profession.

Today, the OMA represents Ontario's physicians, approximately 24,000 in number. It provides insurance and legal services to its members, as well as health services, career information, news of job vacancies and various member benefits such as travel and hotel discounts

It is governed by a Council composed of 250 delegates, representing 78 territorial divisions or branch societies, and by the Association's Board of Directors. The Board consists of representatives from 11 districts, a representative of the six faculties of medicine in Ontario, and five Directors elected by Council.

Headed by the Association's Chief Executive Officer, the OMA has about 160 members of staff who implement policy developed by Council and the Board of Directors. The staff include professionals in the fields of administration, practice management, finance, health policy, legal services, economics, computer technology, insurance, hospital services, laboratory proficiency testing, medical services, physician health, public affairs, and communications.

Jonathan Guss had been hired as the new CEO with some specific directions, namely to bring change and efficiency to the OMA and to do so without raising membership dues. In addition, a new and incredibly complex agreement with the government had created over 30 committees, task forces and working groups in addition to the existing association relationships. He had an energetic change agenda and already had some clear initiatives underway. The Association's key strategic goals were now Renewal (engaging membership), Physician Well-being and a Better Healthcare System for Ontario.

Minna Graham knew Jonathan and so she arranged to meet him to see if she could be helpful in his new role. He thought Minna could provide support to the Professional Services Department and in that very meeting, invited its Executive Director Dr. Michael Thoburn to join the conversation. He was keen to inspire his staff – just a small group in the larger association – and get them energised and innovative about how they could support the reinvention.

The situation

The Professional Services Department is a members' service and includes four areas: Professional Service, Physician Health Program, Rural & Educational Programs and CyberMed. Fourteen people made up the Professional Services team, including administrators, course instructors, web designers, programme coordinators and directors.

Dr. Michael Thoburn was a leader who was sensitive to the dramatic changes that were taking place. He was attuned to the CEO's challenges of working towards renewal of the OMA within a reduced budget. This had already led to a number of changes including the introduction of a performance-based compensation system and a staff reduction scheme eliminating some jobs and consolidating others. In addition to these internal challenges, the Association was beset by detailed and complex negotiations arising from increasingly prescriptive guidelines from government about remuneration for physicians.

This was traumatic for the staff, especially since in making the necessary changes, their purpose was not always made apparent to everyone. Michael was concerned about the impact on his team. Things would be uncertain for a while and people would have to face further changes in direction. But he wanted the group to get excited and contribute to reinventing themselves – what they did and how they did it – in alignment to the strategic goals. He wanted people to think through what would best achieve the strategic direction and how to make best use of their reduced budget and resources to meet members' needs.

The intervention opportunity

The immediate opportunity became clear when the CEO talked about the Leadership Retreat for all of the Executive Directors, including Michael, a month later.

Michael seized that opportunity and asked Minna to facilitate a session with the Professional Services Department. He wanted an idea generation session where the team could develop some clear ideas of what they as a department could offer. Ultimately his goal was to be able to outline and cost some ideas and to apply to the newly set up Innovation Fund where individuals could receive funding for far-reaching projects.

He hoped that the session would generate ideas from the team themselves as well as reflecting on some ideas already being considered (for example, an OMA call centre that would have a full customer relationship management system with the back up of OMA resources). The focus would be on what the different membership groups (students, early practice, mid practice, late practice, residents) would find most valuable.

A staff meeting for all members of the Department was already scheduled for the following week. Given that the Leadership Retreat was one month away, it made sense to start the team thinking process then and then give time for people to digest their early ideas and come back for another solutions focused session in time for the Executive Director to take well-considered thoughts to the Leadership Retreat.

In talking to Michael, it became clear that the functional teams were physically located in different areas of the building and that the team had never met as a whole group before. The OMA Vision and Strategic Goals had been published but it was not clear how many people had seen them and they certainly had not talked about them as a team. Both Michael and Minna wanted the team to have a positive experience. Michael cared deeply about the direction of the group and wanted their innovative ideas. This was a great opportunity to use the Solutions Focused approach.

After this initial meeting, Minna worked directly with Michael and Lisa Harris, the director of Rural & Educational Programs to map out how best to harness the group's energy to focus on the goals.

Positioning of the sessions

The team were told beforehand that the next staff meeting would be led by an outside facilitator. They were told that they would take a positive look at the future and start to build towards it together. The specific session objectives were to:

- Develop a shared view of the Vision and Strategic Goals & gain excitement for the Strategic Plan
- Develop a shared view of team strengths
- Impact Professional Service's future by contributing to the Leadership Retreat
- Discover what the Strategic Plan could mean for them
- Begin to identify what was working and what could be improved
- Decide what to discuss during the second half day session as input to Michael's preparation for the Leadership Retreat.

Word your invitations carefully

Careful wording of the pre-session invitation can be a great help in avoiding confusion and difficulties on the day. We are amazed at how many people put lots of effort into planning a workshop and then neglect to tell people about it. If the participants are not invited in a constructive way they may show up with concerns and confusions, which can take time and effort to deal with.

The First Session

The first session

Welcome and objectives for the day

Things we are most proud of

The Miracle – just imagine

What did we have to be really good at to get there?

Where are we now on a scale of 1 to 7?

What are we already doing to get that high?

Moving up the scale

Impact of today / planning for the second session

Welcome message from Michael

Michael knew that the team were concerned about their future and wanted them to be excited and engaged about it instead and to take control over things they could actually influence. He acknowledged the challenging times and positioned this meeting as a time to look forward, not back. He also outlined the essence of the Vision, Core Values, and Strategic Goals.

Minna reinforced his message by highlighting the session objectives and went directly to an affirming exercise.

Affirmation and appreciation for what they had accomplished so far

Given that the team had not met as a whole and the purpose was to reinvent a future that aligned with Strategic Goals, Minna knew that it was critical that they heard what their colleagues had accomplished. They would be able to see each others' strengths and then later when they looked at their members' needs, they would be well prepared with their strengths well in mind. She says:

> *'As a consultant I think it is important to help teams surface what they have accomplished before they build the future. It is easy for team members to forget, discount or not realise the significance of what they have done. By talking with each other and re-living the details, they create a common context for their achievements and impact and that becomes a foundation from which they can build.'*

This is the exercise she gave them:

Things we are most proud of

I want you to take the next 15 minutes with the colleagues you work with day-to-day to discuss the following topics:

Share a personal success you are most proud of

This could be impact you made through a specific project

It could be how you have grown or become more capable throughout the year

Identify work team success

What were the work team's top two successes and what impact did they have?

What difference did it make to Professional Services, business, the members, or internal clients you serve, and the OMA?

Choose 3 of your stories to share with whole team

The Miracle Question

Energised by stories of success, Minna moved to the Miracle Question, which she expressed as shown in the box below. She asked everyone to come up with as many ideas as possible, each on separate 'post-its.'

Imagine, you go home tonight and when you wake up, it is January two years from now. The latest membership survey headline is on your desk. It says:

'Professional Services seen as corner stone in achieving the OMA Vision and Strategies'.

In addition, the Medical Post is quoted as saying

'Professional Services were the strongest enablers in the organisation. The vision is living and the strategies are humming. Professional services has reinvented itself and all problems have gone away'

What did we do so well to make that happen? How would you know?

What did the survey with members reveal? – What did the members notice that caused such a turnaround? What did medical students notice? Early Practice? Mid Practice? Late Practice? Residents?

What did the interview with the CEO reveal? What did the CEO notice?

What did the government notice?

What did the Professional Services team itself notice was different?

Leap into the future with a time-quake

This kind of Future Perfect exercise is sometimes called a Time-Quake. In the conventional Future Perfect, there is a miracle tonight which suddenly precipitates the arrival of the better future. Here, Minna has chosen a slightly different version where time suddenly passes and things are different. In other aspects the processes are very similar – suppose a better future has arrived, all we have to do is describe it – without wondering overtly about how it came to be. It's good to take care in the Time-Quake (a phrase coined by our colleague John Henden) that the discussion does not slip into 'how to get there'. The development of small steps forward may come later, but is not part of this phase.

What better way to create a passionate view for themselves than the miracle question? The answers gave them a common context, the richness of each others' strengths and accomplishments and enabled them begin to see beyond their own sub teams.

When they had completed their post-it notes, they put them on pre-prepared flip charts categorised by stakeholder perception. If an idea didn't fit under any heading, it was put onto a spare blank 'Orphans' flipchart. Then, everyone stood up and moved around the flipcharts to read them all.

During the debriefing, everyone commented on the themes as they saw them. The themes they identified included

- Centralised resources
- Vocational counselling
- Responsive, timely and relevant
- Sharing information/connectivity
- Professional association is there from student through the whole life cycle and time line
- Helpful friendly 'I will help' proactive attitude
- Easy access to OMA from different points
- Tools to do more
- Negotiations support successful for them
- Members involved in making decisions
- Co-ordinating websites
- Reduced bureaucracy when staff wants to action something
- More use of online facilities
- Delivered as Members want to receive it
- With everything we do, we have POMF- Purpose, objectives, measures and financials

Success Factors, Scaling, and Action Planning

To move towards factors that contribute to excellence, Minna asked another question

'What did we have to be really good at to get there – to realise the vision, strategic goals and our view of the end state?'

People had a few minutes to answer this question for themselves, again using 'post its':

> ## *Expand the Future Perfect with back-casting*
>
> This process is a way of expanding on the Future Perfect discussion. If we know what a better future would look like, what else might be going on to allow it to happen. This kind of process is sometimes called 'back-casting' – enlarging and working around the Future Perfect description to get clearer about the supporting details. Note that this is still very much part of the Future Perfect – this is still in 'imagine the future' territory rather than in looking at what is happening now.

Once they had named the Success Factors, the group decided which were the top four. Everyone chose three items which they thought would have the most impact on the end state. The votes in the right hand column show the votes.

Success Factors to Achieve the End state

Success Factor	Votes
Forecasting and leading to anticipate member needs –'catching the wave' and flexibility to go there	8
Marketing what we do for members	7
Clarity on role of our department in the organization – our focus	7
Strategies of efficiency so it is easy to learn what others do and not spinning in place – how can we know who is doing what and how to connect problem to solution	6
Proactively develop relationships at beginning of their membership	5
Communicate relevant information to members so their call is directed to right resource and the right place	2
Relevant measurable objectives	1

> ### *Just because something's not important doesn't mean it's unimportant*
>
> There were also seven other factors which gained no votes at all. This does not mean they were not important – just not as important as the factors listed above. Having the participants vote in a transparent way shows everyone the support for each item and the relative priorities – and it's much simpler than the facilitator and managers trying to work it out on everyone else's behalf.
>
> Where are we now towards desired state? And 'What are we doing already to get that number?'

Using a 1–7 point scale, with 7 being amazing and 1 being not even on the radar screen, participants were asked to choose a number that represents how well they were doing on each of the top four Success Factors. Collecting counters generated a long list of achievements.

Rating	Success Factor
3	**Forecasting and leading to anticipate member needs –'catching the wave' and having the flexibility to go there** *What are we doing to get to 3?* Professional Development Listening to needs of callers Networking with peers Holding focus groups Program evaluation – constant Research into how well we are meeting needs of specific groups Listening to take direction from government funder

Rating	Success Factor
3	**Marketing what we do for members** *What are we doing to get to 3?* Websites The Ontario Medical Review Some e-mail Fax update Journals Trade show
4	**Clarity on role of our department in the organisation – our focus – Know the core of what we do and what we don't do** *What are we doing to get to 4?* Transferring requests from and to Professional Sevices when appropriate Fairly clear in each department of Professional Services what we do
3.5	**Efficient interconnected communication so we know who is doing what and how to connect problem to solution.** *What are we doing to get to 3.5?* Regular updates Working on common issues

Fit the scaling markers to the situation

The discussion has now finally moved back from the Future Perfect to the current world, with the focus on what is already happening that links forward. Note that Minna's use of a 1–7 scale rather than the traditional 1–10 scale makes not a jot of difference to the process, either in its deployment or its effectiveness.

Moving up the Scale

Next, the group considered the question **'What do we have to do more, better, or different to move one point higher on the scale of 1–7?'**

Success Factor

Forecasting and leading to anticipate member needs –'catching the wave' and flexibility to go there

What do we have to do more, better, or different to get a 4?
Do more of all of the above
Dedicate time for planning
More clarity with objectives and measurements
learn from others- get out there
Translate caller needs onto action plans
Make forecasting/leading a corporate value
Increase OMA articles
Study how to tell them to think differently

Marketing what we do for members

What do we have to do more, better, or different to get a 4?
Showcase Professional Services – common website
Professional Services Newsletter
Internal marketing –gain support internally
Ways to reach physicians without access to web based information – mobile physicians
Road shows
More personal ways to communicate

Clarity on role of our department in the organisation – our focus – know the core of what we do and what we don't do

What do we have to do more, better, or different to get a 5?
When duplication noticed – have a meeting to determine how it happened and how to prevent in future
Having a list of who to call when for what. Sharing each of our lists
When someone calls with multiple problems (overlapping departments) strategise how best to assist caller without multiple calls

Strategies of efficiency so it is easy to learn what others do and not spinning in place – how can we know who is doing what and how to connect problem to solution.
Interconnected Communication

What do we have to do more, better, or different to get a 4.5?
Foster a team mentality
Quarterly updates/ newsletters (email)
Monthly calendar events/presentations, coordination
Professional services Packages
Professional Service website – central face to link
Shared data base of resources for general use

Large steps can lead to small steps

These still seem like quite large steps to us. However, remember the purpose of the session – engaging the people, working together with the strategic plan and creating contributions for the leadership retreat. Minna has worked to achieve these things, and has done so. As we will see the group were keen in any case to move on towards more specifics.

What's next?

Finally, Minna asked the whole group about the impact of this first session together and what they thought would be the best use of the second session.

They thought the best use of their time would be to:

- Get more specific and clearer about the priority ideas and how they align with the Vision and Strategic goals and accelerate progress towards them
- Help Michael represent the message they wanted him to give to the Leadership Retreat as well as possible so that he could best get feedback on the future direction

The Second Session

Michael was delighted by the input of the team members and the first session exceeded his expectations. He considered their work very carefully as he made clear in his invitation to the second session three weeks later. He told them that the session had been excellent and rich in thinking. He had reflected on the output and translated it to Broader Strategic Wants and Priorities to ensure a clear line of sight to the OMA vision and Strategic Goals. Next, he wanted to work on clearer and more concrete definitions of the Professional Services Department's Strategic Wants and how they would meet members needs to guide them to make the best use of current resources.

To prepare for the second session, documentation from the first session as summarised above was given to participants beforehand. Minna asked them to review the notes and in particular to take a look at which ideas most aligned with the vision and strategic goals; which most aligned with what they knew about what their members wanted and which made most sense to do first to give the others a solid foundation. In the light of this, they were asked to choose which of the four success factors they would like to work on further. The second session built on the work of the first meeting, using similar SF processes.

The outcome

Michael found the work very productive in raising employee engagement. He said the feedback from staff was terrific; they felt that their opinions and ideas were respected and appreciated. This is confirmed by Lisa Harris, Director of Rural and Educational Programs who says

> 'These were two very productive sessions, the feedback from the staff was terrific. They felt their opinions and ideas were respected and appreciated.'

Since the meetings, Michael has moved to the same floor as his staff (away from the 'top team' floor). His staff perceive this as a good thing and the CEO sees him as a champion in this respect.

The main and lasting value of Minna's work was the team's heightened awareness of each other's strengths. It let people see their work as key to achieving the OMA Strategic Plan goals; this too increased their confidence. Michael thought the intervention was successful in getting the team to be ready to move ahead. People could look beyond their day-to-day concerns and become more aware of the context in which they worked and the direction the organisation was heading for.

Michael told us that

'It got people thinking about what they did and what they could do and prompted an awareness which really served us well. This awareness led to increased confidence and idea generation with a willingness to think outside the box. People do what they believe in, what they understand and what they're paid to do.'

In addition,

'The meetings helped me do an inventory of my staff, to see them interact, to see who bubbled to the top and to prepare me for the CEO's onslaught.'

Other members of the department said

'We feel more like a team now.'

'We realise that as a team, we have a variety of ways we can support our members'

'It was very helpful to be able to think about the strategic direction and how we can make an impact.'

Minna Graham of Focused Design Inc is a consultant passionately committed to leadership development, team performance, and organisational effectiveness. She designs and facilitates sessions that demonstrate her gently relentless focus on helping her clients build shared accountability and commitment to achieving business results.

Minna Graham, Focused Design Inc
281 Indian Road, Toronto, Ontario M6R 2X4, Canada
+ 01 416 535 1945
minna.focuseddesign@sympatico.ca

Chapter 4

Turning the tables on quality

Solutions Focus meets continuous improvement at Sky

Co-author: Trevor Durnford

Organisation: British Sky Broadcasting Group

Traditional continuous improvement processes are usually highly problem focused. In this fascinating story from a leading broadcasting organisation the introduction of Solutions Focused ideas alongside more conventional approaches, including Six Sigma, produces benefits and surprises which challenge much conventional wisdom.

British Sky Broadcasting Group (referred to here as Sky) is the operator of the UK's leading digital television service and a leading broadcaster of sports, movies, entertainment and news. Since its creation just 18 years ago, Sky has changed the face of entertainment with more than 8 million households throughout the UK and Ireland enjoying a vast choice of programmes across 400 channels. As well as providing a digital satellite broadcasting service, it also supplies and maintains set-top boxes and manages subscriptions for millions of customers in the UK.

During its short history, Sky has grown from an operation that employed just a handful of people to a household name that employs 13,000 and has a turnover of £3.7 billion. So it is not surprising that the culture in Sky is one where fast paced innovation thrives.

In the spring of 2004, Edwina McDowall, Technical Services Director, contacted Trevor Durnford at Kaizen Training to explore how to adopt a culture of 'continuous improvement' where people at the workplace are actively engaged in enhancing their own work. Sky had worked with Kaizen Training before and knew that they were familiar with Sky's culture and values. She liked Kaizen Training's flexible approach and their ability to be welcoming and inviting to people from different backgrounds.

Before embarking on a broad roll-out across the contact centres, Edwina was keen to develop some 'quick wins' which could be used as a proof of concept and provide confidence that the broader adoption of the Kaizen philosophy would bring about the desired change. In particular, she wanted to see an improvement in business processes brought about by the involvement of those close to the workplace.

This process has been branded 'Sky Kaizen'. The development of a Solutions Focused approach allied to more conventional continuous improvement methods was a key part of the change process at Sky. This chapter describes:

- How SF was adopted in the early pilot project
- SF thinking in the diagnostic phase and in the broad change process roll-out
- The development of in house Kaizen Facilitators in SF tools
- Examples of successful SF applications at Sky

Kaizen, DMAIC and Six Sigma

Kaizen is an approach to productivity improvement with origins in Japan. The word is usually translated into English as continuous improvement, and relates to a whole range of activities designed to enhance productivity, effectiveness and efficiency at work. Kaizen Training is also the name of the organisation for which Trevor works.

Six Sigma is a proprietary framework for quality improvement. Based on statistical measurements, the tools of Six Sigma help the users eliminate variability, defects and waste that undermine customer loyalty. One of the key tools in Six Sigma is the DMAIC approach to problem solving:

- **Define** the process improvement goals that are consistent with customer demands and enterprise strategy.
- **Measure** the current process and collect relevant data for future comparison.

- **Analyse** to verify relationship and causality of factors. Determine what the relationship is, and attempt to ensure that all factors have been considered.
- **Improve** or optimise the process in line with the analysis
- **Control** to ensure that any variances are corrected before they result in defects. Set up pilot runs to establish process capability, transition to production and thereafter continuously measure the process and institute control mechanisms.

Solutions Focus can work alongside problem focus

The DMAIC framework clearly stems from a different tradition to SF. However, it has been found very effective when applied to the right kinds of topic. This case will show how SF ideas can be used with problem-focused approaches like DMAIC, as well as an alternative route.

The name Six Sigma was chosen in recognition of an exemplary high quality standard. Sigma is the Greek letter given to the standard deviation parameter in statistics – a measure of the amount of variation in a given population. The developers of Six Sigma were aiming for a quality standard in which the operation of a manufactured component would only be compromised if the quality was more than six standard deviations – Six Sigma – from the average. This gives an aspirational defect level of 3.4 per million – a very small number indeed.

The Pilot

Edwina wanted to try out the approach in a well-defined area, where the approach would be well tested and she could clearly show the results. She chose a topic called 'No Fault Found' (NFF). This was a regular item at meetings and one of the three or four topics taking up most of her time. In this situation, a customer contacts Sky because their set top box doesn't seem to be working properly. The field engineer can't find what's wrong with it and returns it to the box repair centre – and there, in almost half of the cases, it seems to work perfectly. Not only is this hugely frustrating for all involved, it wastes time, energy and materials and has a negative impact on customer satisfaction. With hard costs at nearly £150k per week, this was a good test case – very specific, with measurable results.

A cross functional team including people from the Service and Repair Department, Field Engineers, the Technical Contact Centre and the Repair Centre was formed to tackle this problem using the Kaizen approach. Trevor Durnford facilitated the team.

Trevor introduced the group to the principles of Kaizen and the DMAIC 'problem solving' framework and set about helping the group develop its project charter to answer most of the basic questions about outcomes, ways of working and assumptions. In parallel, he introduced the team to the principles of Solutions Focused working. The group started by mapping the existing process in detail and building a 'dash board' that highlighted the overall process metrics. Faults were more than four orders of magnitude away from the Six Sigma ideal of 3.4 defects per million opportunities.

The team then worked together over a period of 2 months meeting for a full day every 2 weeks or so to develop recommendations and take action that would improve the situation. Whilst DMAIC proved helpful in helping the group to measure the size of the problem (and therefore how (really) bad the situation was), the real breakthrough came when the Solutions Focus was applied to the situation. The team asked themselves if there was anywhere in the company where the field engineers were consistently able to diagnose and repair systems without having to send them to the repair centre. This was a search for counters to the problem – examples of something more like the success that Sky wanted all its teams to achieve.

The search for counters revealed a small team in the south of England that seemed to perform exceptionally well in this area. Trevor went to see team Leader Adrian Manson and some of his people to ask how they managed so well, despite having the same training and resources as their colleagues elsewhere in the company. The key difference was that Adrian's team kept an informal 'league table' amongst the engineers and the competition amongst them did the rest! The rollout of this league table across the UK formed a key part of the team's recommendations.

The team members were impressed with the approach and felt it would be a valuable part of a tool kit for future projects. They found it a very refreshing alternative resulting in creative answers which would not have been found using a problem solving approach. Previously, conversation in the contact centre was about things not working, so this created a useful alternative.

> ## Change interactions by creating alternative conversations
>
> In an interactional view, organisations can be looked at as the sum of their conversations. In this case it is not surprising that changing conversations can change organisations.

Solutions Focus – reversing back to quality

Trevor says:

> *'Keeping the SF approach as a separate conversation from the DMAIC framework was a key to its success, but it also proved that the two approaches CAN be used on the same project.'*

Any of the conventional tools of quality improvement can be given a Solutions Focused twist, with great results. For example, in a clever reversal of the 6–sigma fishbone diagram, Trevor has introduced Future Perfect at the head of the fish, with counters and back casting questions forming the skeleton.

Conventional fishbone	SF fishbone – Wishbone
Be sure everyone agrees on the effect or problem statement before starting	Be sure everyone agrees on the ideal outcome before starting
Be succinct	Be succinct.
For each node, think what could be its causes. Add them to the tree	Working backwards from the head, think about what might help to achieve each node. Add the possibilities to the tree.
Pursue each line of causality back to its root cause	Pursue each promising line back to small initiating steps
Consider grafting relatively empty branches onto others	Consider grafting relatively empty branches onto others.
Consider splitting up over-crowded branches	Consider splitting up over crowded branches.
Consider which root causes are most likely to merit further investigation	Consider which small steps are most likely to merit further investigation.

> ### *Solutionise your tool box*
>
> There are many other potential applications of this kind of reversal. These are all potential applications of our maxim about focusing on what you want and what helps you achieve it, rather than what you don't want and what's stopping you from getting something better.

SF in the roll-out planning phase

Trevor recommended that prior to any larger scale roll-out of the approach, the 'mood' of the business should be gauged. This was another opportunity to apply some of the SF principles.

Seventy-four people representing a cross section of people from across Sky were invited to take part in focus group discussions facilitated by Trevor. The sessions began with a brief overview of what a Kaizen culture could be like. To check whether this future (as defined by Edwina McDowall and her executive colleagues) was really desirable in the minds of the participants, they were each asked to comment on the statement that 'the business does not really need Continuous Improvement/Kaizen at this time' – 92% disagreed with this statement

The groups were also asked 'What could work in our favour?' with responses including good internal training resource, gossip and rumour (as opposed to large scale broadcasting of corporate message and initiatives).

These views influenced the design of the roll-out of Kaizen at Sky and it was kept very low key in the early months. The feeling was that curiosity and interest would be stimulated if things were discussed as more of a 'rumour' than a mandated initiative. Many such initiatives had come and gone and the request from those in the focus groups was very much along the lines of 'keep it low key, don't give us the usual posters, mouse-mats and rah-rah'. Sky advertised internally for facilitators to work on the beginnings of something – something not really specified. Numbers were restricted to 50 – and 300 people applied! This demonstrates the power of rumour and of a feeling of scarcity – both intriguing motivators in this case. Appetites were further whetted by an article in the in-house newsletter about the NFF project. Out of the 50, just over half became active after their training, giving a small number of Sky people working on improvement.

A year later, the focus groups met again with many of the same people involved. Trevor was intrigued to notice that:

'the message was clear ... 'Why are you keeping this a secret ... everyone should be involved and engaged''!

The learning from using SF in the planning phase was:

- People throughout the business will be able to come up with organisational 'counters'– things which would help in this particular context.
- Received wisdom and textbook approaches can be cast aside in favour of what has worked and what hasn't.

Trevor says:

'Most Kaizen or Continuous Improvement text books would advocate that this type of change 'must come from the top' and must be communicated X 10 before real progress can be made .... .this is bunkum!'

Some 18 months after the first pilot project, Sky embarked on a major internal marketing and communication campaign, which was received much more positively than previous attempts.

Technical Services Director Edwina McDowall says

'Kaizen really is the fabric of our business'.

Start slowly and avoid resistance

There is an SF adage 'if you want to go fast, go slow'. 'Resistance' sets in when people feel that someone else is forcing the pace – even if it's in a direction they want to go! This is one of the reasons why we don't insist on high level support for initiatives. People can be very inventive at sabotaging initiatives that seem to be imposed on them. Change can start anywhere.

The Development of Kaizen Facilitators

With the client positively disposed towards a combination of a 'problem solving' approach based on DMAIC and SF, the next step was to begin training internal Kaizen facilitators. The champions of change were selected from over 300 volunteers.

Trevor was amazed by the initial response.

'Our early conversations were more about what to do if we only get ten or so volunteers stepping forward when the client is keen to develop 50. There are now 140 trained facilitators in Sky!'

An early distinction was made between a 'Kaizen Team' and a 'Kaizen Project'. The former being an ongoing improvement activity involving a natural work-team, the latter being a cross functional/departmental project with a specified time frame.

Suzanne Stannard, in charge of the Kaizen roll-out at Sky, is keen to point out the benefits of getting a project team together intensively over three to five days. The teams looked at specific aspects like absence and attrition (high staff turnover). Taking a particular topic had a great benefit, making space for people to explore issues outside their normal environment.

Kaizen Project Facilitators were trained in both DMAIC and SF tools and techniques. A 3 day participative and experiential workshop introduced the facilitators to Solutions Focus thinking and methods. The workshop included what to focus on and what to overlook, the difference between problem focused and solution focused questioning, exploring the Future Perfect and scaling – using the Scaling Walk devised by Paul Z Jackson. More recently, 30 people have decided to join a year long Blackbelt programme for Sky Kaizen facilitators.

Suzanne comments on the importance of support for the facilitators in the early stages.

'Things that help the facilitators stay involved include having a clear area to address at the outset. We've enlisted support from managers in addressing this and have been more directive in our approach asking managers to meet up with their facilitators before attending the training to give the facilitators a purpose, a real challenge in the workplace that they could help teams with. We found that being more directive at the start was helpful, and we do more of this now than we did early in the project.'

Empower Hour

To give the facilitators an opportunity to support each other with difficult situations, the company has been using the Solutions Focused Reflecting Team process (see for example Norman, Hjerth and Pidsley 2005). Suzanne Stannard:

'We now have some 200 facilitators and only a couple of support people internally, so we can't give as much individual coaching time to each facilitator as we'd like. We got the facilitators together and shared the SFRT process and came out with idea of the Empower Hour. Coaching for facilitators can be a self-maintained process, with a lead facilitator for each team to help people stick to the process. Groups of six to eight facilitators meet for an hour each month to bring issues and get input. This also serves as a chance for people to network.

'The groups share their various issues and vote for which issues should get time for formal discussion. I've seen people come along with a challenge and walk away with four or five sheets of A4 full of ideas about what they could do, as well as appreciations of what they are doing already. They get a lot of ideas and inspiration in a small amount of time.'

Project Successes

Billings Process

Early in the Sky Kaizen roll-out, a project was launched with the daunting task of improving the entire billings process, with Trevor's colleague Alastair Olby facilitating. Using 'problem solving' root cause analysis, the project team were surprised to discover that one area to explore further was staff education. Mistakes were being made in the billings process because incorrect promotional codes were being used and so call centres didn't always have the right information to hand.

When the team explored the question using a billings quiz, 'where do we perform best in handling billings calls?' the answer was Sky's call centre in India. This was a surprise to the team as conventional wisdom says that outsource partners generally underperform. What seemed to set them apart included a thirst to learn, a high level of education (all graduates), and for many, recent training as they had not been with Sky for long. It was also found that Customer Advisors (CAs) were able to calculate bills well when the billings calculator came to the fore of the screen when they changed something mid-month. Conversely, when the technology didn't let the CA see the calculator and complex calculations had to be done, call times would go up and/or the wrong information would be given and/or the CA couldn't give the customer what they wanted. The existing system didn't show the calculator for the really difficult calculations at all, doing it all behind the scenes and giving the CA an end figure only. This became an obvious recommendation from the project team. Training in the Scotland call centre has been reviewed. It now includes a quiz 'Who wants to be a BILLionaire?' which leads to debate between teams, flags up areas of confusion and inconsistencies – and is fun!

Induction Process

The process of inducting new people into Sky also became the target of a Kaizen Project team. The team first looked at all the things that were working well in the 'old' system to identify and affirm those counters and make sure they were kept in the new programme. The team then looked at where induction seemed to be working really well and uncovered a project at the head office site where a completely new sales team called project Deva had been established. Training managers who worked on the Induction Project were dispatched to London where there was an isolated area offering a new model, with new thinking and new practice to go with it. Their task was to find out what had worked there.

Search widely for counters

This wider search for counters beyond the horizon is a very useful twist. 'Where does something similar to what we want already happening?' is a useful question to ask.

The managers noticed that new starters in Deva were firstly trained in the products (for example different programme packages, broadband, telephone etc) and types of people that used them, followed by an introduction to communication and relationship skills. Only then were the new recruits introduced to the business processes. This was a radical departure from the standard approach adopted by Sky which introduced people to business processes first.

The 'Deva' format for induction training formed a key part of the team's recommendations and the pilot results have been astounding. Before the improvement, the quality of a new starters' call handling shortly after their induction ranged from 37% to 93%, the first pilot which incorporated the new way of induction training has shown that this figure ranges from 93% to 100%. Further courses following the new model are planned.

The inconsistent turnover rates for contact centre staff within different business areas was also investigated, and turned out also to have some connection to staff induction. Suzanne Stannard recalls that the turnover rate in engineering was much lower than other areas, so a team investigated the differences. What did engineering do that the contact centre didn't? The team discovered a much longer induction in engineering compared to the intensive 2–3 weeks in the contact centre. Not only was it longer, but different – a self managed process with workbooks and tasks to discover information from within the organisation. A revised induction process in the contact centres is being piloted, and the initial response has been good.

Call Handling Guidelines

One of the main tensions in a contact centre environment is how to encourage CAs to have real conversations with customers and at the same time ensure that they provide a service that consistently delights customers.

One approach has been to provide contact centre teams with Call Handling Guidelines. The intention of these guidelines is simply to provide a framework within which CAs can operate rather than a set of rules and regulations. A team was established to look at why these guidelines were being adopted to varying degrees.

The team explored:

o **When** are the guidelines being applied consistently
o **When** are the guidelines **NOT** being applied consistently
o **Where** are the guidelines being applied consistently
o **Where** are the guidelines **NOT** being applied consistently
o **What** guidelines are being applied consistently
o **What** guidelines are **NOT** being applied consistently
o **How** do we know the guidelines are being applied consistently
o **How** do we know the guidelines are **NOT** being applied consistently
o **Why** are the guidelines being applied consistently
o **Why** are the guidelines **NOT** being applied consistently

The 'NOT' brainstorms were put to one side so the group could focus on the elements that helped when it was working ... the counters. Previously, they had focused solely on the NOTs – leading to a huge tome which no-one ever consulted!

The team found that the guidelines seemed to be used most appropriately:

- In small teams
- When a guidelines expert was in the area
- In areas that shared the same building as the guideline developers.

Find the 'why' of what's wanted, not what's wrong

Some people think that Why questions are banned in the SF world. A Why directed to an analysis of what's working or what needs to work – like in the Wishbone model – may well be fruitful.

And as a result the team that develops the guidelines have been working extensively to raise their profile and face to face interaction in the call centres. Following this interaction, they are now in the process of simplifying the guidelines yet further.

Generating new possibilities

Suzanne Stannard has been impressed with the application of SF ideas within the project.

> 'It can be a tendency to focus on the problem and take a negative line of questioning. SF has really helped to put people into a more creative frame of mind and come up with things they might not have considered.'

Suzanne recalls a particular project team working in the contact centre:

> 'The team had made some successful changes, and then regrouped to work out how to sustain them. There was a long silence from the team. Alistair (the Kaizen Training facilitator) asked them 'think about things that are already sustained, what helped them to be sustained ... '. It got people out of the stuck rut, into some positive ideas – for example knowledge management systems, call handling guidelines, the things that we always have to do ... and what about that that really keeps them going. Then the ideas started to come. The group went from being stuck to a new line of thought.'

Trevor's Reflections

The use of SF principles at Sky has proved invaluable in helping the successful roll-out of a major whole systems change process. In addition, at a micro level, the improvement teams that have been launched have also enjoyed some success in using the principles with results beginning to emerge.

Trevor says that for him the key learning has been that

> *'SF and Problem solving approaches can be used in the same project (although very definitely NOT at the same time). Nobody told us this, it just seemed sensible not to. As facilitators, it's so we can get our heads straight. Change of focus is considerable, and keeping the approaches separate avoids confusion – we change after coffee or a break. We would shift focus when something going on in the room lets the facilitator know that it's a good time to move to SF – eg when the state seems hopeless or when DMAIC has not produced something radical or interesting.'*

Other key learnings:

- The change in team morale as a result of focusing on what works (when their usual conversation is what's wrong and how has it got so bad) is massive
- Be prepared to throw out text book wisdom regarding change processes when 'what works' has been uncovered. – Keep it simple.

Suzanne Stannard agrees:

> *'There is merit in a gentle soft launch to the project. We found lots of instances where people had heard the name, started getting interested and wanted to find out more. Letting the word spread naturally and at a pace driven by need, rather than forcing the issue, has been a good learning for us.'*

References:

Harry Norman, Michael Hjerth and Tim Pidsley, Solution Focused Reflecting Teams in Action, in 'Positive Approaches to Change' (Mark McKergow and Jenny Clarke, eds), SolutionsBooks (2005)

Thorana Nelson (ed.): Education and Training in Solution Focused Brief Therapy, Haworth Press.(2006)

Trevor Durnford is a member of the Kaizen Training Ltd. team and has a track record of working throughout the world with organisations implementing major change projects. His extensive success in helping organisations change is backed up by 20 years in business, with directorships in HR and Change for large global companies. Trevor is a Certified Professional Facilitator, accredited by the IAF and is a real advocate for 'brain friendly learning'.

trevor@kaizen-training.com
+44 7966 753565

Chapter 5

Back to the future

Increasing sales with positive differences

Co-authors: Kathrin Bauer and Günter Lueger

Organisation: Magazzin

Sales figures were falling at a family-owned sports and leisure wear business. What was to be done? Examine the reasons for the fall, or examine positive differences to produce new ideas and strategies? This latter process had impacts not just on sales, but also on the owners and staff.

Kathrin Bauer is one of the owners and managing director of Magazzin, a family business selling sports and leisure wear through two shops in the centre of Graz, Austria. Kathrin's parents started the firm in 1972, selling a range of sports equipment including skis, fishing equipment and surfboards. By 2004, Kathrin's mother was simply selling clothes; the market had changed, and there were more opportunities in sports and leisure wear. She had also expanded to a second shop nearby, a franschise operation selling clothes chosen by the Bauers from the range of a single popular manufacturer. The shops occupy good sites – the main Magazzin shop is near the cathedral, while the franchise shop is near to the main shopping street.

When Kathrin joined the family firm in 2004 she found that sales had been slipping in both shops during the previous couple of years. She was particularly concerned with the franchise shop, which was showing an eight percent reduction in sales over the past year.

Kathrin went to discuss the situation with Dr Günter Lueger of NextTools, Vienna. She already knew the SF approach quite well, having discovered it during her training in systemic structural constellations with Matthias Varga von Kibéd and Insa Sparrer. As an experienced SF consultant and coach, Günter was keen to apply the approach to this situation.

The effectiveness of the approach in dealing with people issues like appraisal was not in doubt. However, having worked in the financial department of a big Austrian telecommunications company, Kathrin was more sceptical about using the SF approach to tackle financial issues. She and Günter agreed to work together on the issue in a modest way – with just two 90 minute coaching sessions.

First coaching session

At the first coaching session Günter asked Kathrin to bring along any materials, paperwork and figures that she thought might be relevant. At the start of the process Günter asked how she would know that the consulting had been helpful to her. She replied that an increase in the sales figures was important for her; something had to be done, particularly about the franchise outlet where sales were falling fast. The family had discussed the problem on many occasions over a long period of time. They had tried to find concrete steps to take, but nothing seemed to make sense in tackling the issue. So, finding some sensible concrete steps was also important.

Then Kathrin described the background to the sales decline and concentrated on talking about the problematic franchise outlet. She went into detail about some of the contributing factors to the problem; the outlet manager (who ran the shop on the family's behalf) did not get on well with her mother and behaved in a difficult way sometimes, and the employees were less motivated. In addition there was a lot of construction work going on in the street outside the shop, which was a nuisance and put people off coming in.

The 'solution' is not the opposite of the problem

These things could be said to be the cause of the problem. Some might be tractable and within Kathrin's sphere of influence. Others (like the construction work) seem to be outside her control. However, remember that the solution – what is wanted – is independent of the problem . . .

Günter moved the conversation in a Solutions Focused way, asking about the differences between the two shops by focusing on the one where things were better. In the Magazzin shop there was a slight increase in sales during the last year. It was not easy for Kathrin to concentrate on this shop – many times she moved her attention back to the negative things in the problematic outlet. However, she gradually discovered a lot of useful differences concerning the better shop – things which she described later as very helpful.

Günter's questions were along these lines:

- What would you say is different in the outlet where things are better?
- How do you recognise moments at work when things are a little bit better?
- How come the sales figures are higher in this shop?
- If I asked the most skillful or most experienced employee, what would he/she say that is different in the more successful shop?
- If I asked one of your best customers, what would he/she say that is different ...
    - in the successful outlet in comparison to the other one? And – what would she/say that is different in the problematic outlet when things are better there?

Kathrin:

'The questions about how the other people would see the shop were very helpful. I had the feeling that I went into my shop looking through new eyes. It was very helpful later on when I organised a rebuilding of the shop. I had all these pictures in my mind, and could see right away how things should be.'

Positive differences come from many comparisons

There is an impressive array of questions in action here. Positive differences are sought both in general and 'in the moment'. The perspectives of employees and customers are sought, and specifically those who might know the shops best. The last question presents the idea that there may also be traces of positive difference in the problematic shop – a point which will be brought out further later.

Kathrin's answers to this range of questions encapsulated some key positive differences:

- In the successful outlet more people come into the shop not simply to buy, but also to chat with the employees. (Kathrin saw this as very helpful, not as a negative – it gives the staff the chance to show off their latest stock.) This was helped by the outgoing personality of one of the staff members
- The furniture was different in this outlet – it looks more like a living room
- Brightness in the outlets is important – lighting and a bright feel
- The display in the shop window makes a difference
- Decisions on stock purchasing made in consultation rather than by individuals, with people involved in buying particular stock that they themselves wear and know about
- More motivation of the staff by fostering a feeling that both outlets are one team (more participation in joint meetings)
- Handling conflicts is more useful than avoiding them
- Different information flow with the franchise-company (more open-minded)

Günter: 'This is an excellent example of how there is no connection between the problem and the solution. When Kathrin was talking about the problematic shop she talked about behaviour problems and the construction work outside the shop. She didn't talk about the furniture and the gossip associated with the better shop. These are not the opposites of construction work! There is a new quality of information in the discussion of the positive differences – more detailed as well as different.'

The gossip in the Magazzin shop provided a very fruitful source of information. The atmosphere was different. Regulars came in after their holidays to talk about their adventures. It was like a living room. Part of this environment was created by the fact that the staff stood at the same physical level as the customers; the counter in the other shop was raised by about 30cm and was approached by a step, which did not allow the same kind of gossip and relations with customers. The Magazzin shop was lighter, more open, had more room to move.

> ### *Every case is different*
>
> The number of different aspects of the shop which emerged from the discussion about gossip is an excellent example of the maxim 'Every case is different'. We are not sure how many retail manuals describe the importance of gossip – it would not seem to be key to success in every retail environment. And yet, here it is.

Günter continued his questions by looking more closely at the sales figures:

- Take the sales figures and gross profit margin for the problematic outlet and transfer them onto a sheet of paper. How did the figures change over time? (Kathrin drew a line through the figures and there were some positive differences). What was different during the periods of higher sales?
- Examine the gross profit margin figures for both shops. What can you recognise as an important development that you could use now?
- Look at the figures of your company in comparison to the competition. What is better in your company and how can you use that now?

This starts to get at difference **within** the performance of each individual shop. For example, sales in the problematic outlet were 10% higher in certain periods the previous year than at the time of the coaching. How come? Factors included the involvement of the family in the purchasing decisions (which were better with their involvement), more advertisements (July is a sale month), big reductions on sale items, a final sale (everything reduced by 50%), and only selling the items they want to get rid of (keeping the items with continuing shelf life in the back until after the sale).

Günter: *'I was again amazed at the quantity of detailed and positive information that Kathrin was able to produce, almost instantly. I used the tactic of going with the flow of concrete information that emerged and picking out the positive differences for closer examination. For example, when it emerged that the furniture in the better outlet is different, I first asked about the details and then the differences concerning the furniture (like:*

what would the best customer say is important about how the furniture helps sales in certain parts of the shop? How about the most motivated employee? And so on.'

Different perspectives give different details

Small details are very important in Solutions Focused work. Interestingly, the small details noticed by one person may be different to those noticed by another. What is remarkable is that Kathrin can produce different perspectives simply by being asked – even though she is still the same person. This is not at all unusual, and shows the importance of exploring what's working from different viewpoints.

Working directly with the family and employees

Between the two coaching sessions, Kathrin called a workshop meeting with the employees. She used SF facilitation and preparation, to lead the questioning in a similar way to the first coaching session.

First she sat down with her mother and sister (the active owner / managers of the shops at that time) with the same questions and figures, looking for differences when the revenue was higher. They examined purchasing, advertising and window displays, among many other things. One conclusion was that changes in furniture could be key in moving things forwards – changing the height of the counter in the franchise shop, for example. The session produced a great deal of shared understanding, as well as good ideas. It also emerged that Kathrin's mother was coming under pressure from the franchise partner to halt the slide in sales by moving to a bigger shop. This was difficult in practice: bigger shops are not easy to find and are more expensive. In any case, improvements were needed fast.

Kathrin then convened a workshop with all the employees from the two shops, as well as her mother and sister. She again presented the financial results, and then sought help from the employees in looking for differences. When a customer comes in, what is different when they have a good experience in the shop? What helps you to sell the clothes, what helps you to discover the customer's wants and wishes? What is different when revenue is higher – with the stock, advertising, window display, customer service, tailoring (alterations) and approval service (customers can take clothes home to try on). They wrote down their ideas and sorted them by category.

Many of the same ideas emerged as when Kathrin had discussed the issue with her family. However, the staff were engaged in the process and started to give a lot of support to the proposed ideas. This increase in energy came during the discussion, not as a precursor to it.

Use incidental energy

Some methodologies advocate getting into a good 'state' prior to working on problems. Using SF ideas you will find again and again that people's energy to work on things increases as the conversation progresses. There is no need to separately 'change state' before starting work.

Kathrin helped everyone to prioritise the ideas by using sticky dots. Everyone had a small sheet of sticky dots and applied them to what they thought were the most important ideas. Then everyone could see the relative views on what's important, and put small steps in place. One of the ideas was 'We should all laugh and smile – even when Mrs X (who is a bit of a nuisance) comes into the shop.' Now, of course, when Mrs X does come in, they all make a special effort to laugh. Other small steps included finding new outfits all together in the shop, and to call regular customers when new products arrived.

Second coaching session

The second ninety minute coaching session took place two months after the first. The focus was on:

- what worked well in the workshops
- how Kathrin could recognise that things had already started to change
- scaling the different activities to examine confidence that they could contribute to an increase in sales
- asking for details that could be the next steps.

Then Kathrin agreed the next steps with her family and started to implement them: she started to refit the franchise shop, began a different product policy and encouraged everyone to take the steps they had identified together.

Reflections on the project

Two years later, turnover in the franchise shop is 20% higher. The Magazzin shop is also running well, with 5 % higher sales. There have been other benefits too – the franchise shop manager is now keen to know what she can do better for Kathrin (she had always been very problem focused), and the tension between her and the owners is no longer an issue. Motivation among all the staff has improved. Kathrin is very satisfied with all this.

Kathrin: *'It was a surprise that during the process with my mother and sister, there was no discussion about the costs of improving the shops. We all knew that we would do it, the only question was how. And I always had confidence that this would work, and that I could manage it. The 'solution' (what we wanted) was so clear that I never had any doubts. I am very pleased with the sales increases, particularly in view of the fact that the local market is getting more difficult – a competing shop has opened nearby. My sister is now more involved with the purchasing, and the atmosphere is better in the shops.'*

Günter: *'It is particularly interesting in this case that Kathrin was so clear about how she wanted the shops to be, and absolutely confident that she could do it – and yet I never asked her a miracle question or to describe a Future Perfect. She has come to all this knowledge just from looking at the positive differences. Also, we did not use scaling, in the conventional SF way of a scale from 1 – 10. The financial figures served as one basis for conversations about differences without the need for further scales.'*

Know the end in detail – however you can.

George Mallory, the leading English mountaineer of the early 20th century, once wrote 'You must know the end in order to win the end'. SF practice clearly incorporates this idea in various ways – usually by using the Future Perfect tool. What is interesting in this case is how simple discussions of positive difference seem to have had the same effect.

In discussing the project, Kathrin realised that, although the motivation of staff was better now and lack of motivation was part of the problem, there had been no work on 'motivation' as part of the project. The increased motivation is a natural part of the other changes. Günter comments:

'This reflects the Interactional View which is a fundamental part of SF practice. Motivation is an interactional phenomenon, not a property of an individual. We often speak of 'increasing someone's motivation', but a more honest way to see it is to think of putting people into situations where they will naturally be more motivated. The increase in motivation is a natural result of the other changes, and never needed to be a centre of attention in itself. This is a good example of the motto 'Don't change someone, change something' '

Don't change some*one,* change some*thing*

We are often asked about how to change other people. This is very difficult. It gets easier, however, when you start to investigate times when the desired behaviour happens anyway. Motivation, like other emotions, is not an absolute – it is rooted inextricably in contexts and occasions. Talking about it in other ways or even trying to measure it is to risk a philosophical – and practical – muddle. Changing something – connected to motivation – is simpler than trying to change someone's motivation as if it was no more difficult than changing their shirt.

Günter reflects on the way in which financial figures proved such a useful basis for a solution focused discussion in this case:

'Management information systems are full of information about facts and figures. And yet they are not used to provide information on positive differences. There is a lot of potential in devising and implementing new ways to show management information, to be clearer about these positive differences and make them open for management decision making.'

Kathrin Bauer is manger and co-owner of Magazzin. She worked in the financial department of a large Austrian telecommunication company and trained in systemic structural constellations with Matthias Varga von Kibéd and Insa Sparrer. Kathrin Bauer uses the SF approach in her daily management work in contact with employees, customers, suppliers and with financial information.

Günter Lueger is a director of NextTools and has developed SF management instruments like Solution-Focused Assessment, SF-Rating and the NextToolBox based on the theory of positive differences. He lectures internationally and writes articles and books about the transfer of SF prinicples into different fields of management. He supports companies to redesign their management instruments to find the difference that makes a difference to their success.

Pokornygasse 27/7
A-1190 Vienna
Austria
0043 1 3694523
Mail: lueger@nexttools.net
Web: www.nexttools.net

Chapter 6

Making sense of information:

Developing a patient-friendly framework for hospital planning

Co-author: Peter Röhrig

Organisation: The Cologne Local Health Conference
(Kommunale Gesundheitskonferenz Köln)

The clients thought they would get expert advice; the consultant confounded their expectations by encouraging their own expertise to emerge. How the SF approach helped a working group make sense of a mass (mess!) of information and produce a coherent, structured report to develop the German hospital system.

The Cologne Local Health Conference (Kommunale Gesund-heitskonferenz Köln or KGK) is a local committee of representatives of health care professionals and users charged with using local knowledge to make recommendations to improve health care and promotion in Cologne, a city of about 1 million people, with 2 million in the wider metropolitan area.

In July 2003 the KGK decided to appoint a working group to look into hospital planning. It was commissioned to look at hospital design from the patients' perspective and compile a list of relevant planning guidelines. The group consisted of representatives from social groups affected by hospital planning, including senior citizens, migrants, self help groups and parents. Two professionals led the group, Yvonne Oertel, manager of the Cologne Centre for Self Help Groups (KISS) and Wolfgang Klier, CEO of the KGK.

The working group met regularly for more than two years, inquiring into

- The kind of upsetting situations people experienced during their stay in hospital
- The main complaints made by patients
- The special needs and interests of different patient groups

During this period they learned about the most frequent and annoying problems encountered by different patient groups in hospitals. Migrants reported for instance, that doctors and nurses could not understand them properly and asked for translation facilities. Parents complained about the lack of opportunity to stay with their children. Senior citizens wanted better recognition of the social environment of elderly people before discharging them from hospital etc. Lots of ideas and suggestions emerged.

A mass of mess

Information gathering was easy and the group worked well together. However, the task became more difficult when they tried to find similarities among all the suggestions in order to frame more general guidelines. Yvonne and Wolfgang looked for help in hospitals' quality reports and consulted an expert in hospital planning. This led to even more data and more confusion and they needed help in making a coherent story out of it all.

Yvonne recalls:

'We had lots of ideas, stories and examples from the various groups. Their experience was very different and it was difficult to see how to make a coherent report from it all. The hospital quality reports and the hospital planning expert just added to the wealth of information – we still couldn't see how to structure it all usefully.'

Peter Röhrig was known to the KGK and well respected for his experience and knowledge of the health care sector. When Yvonne and Wolfgang first contacted him in September 2005, they sent him a huge pile of paper, hundreds of pages full of all sorts of information and ideas. They asked him to help them produce a structured catalogue of guidelines.

The first meeting

Peter worked only with Yvonne and Wolfgang – he did not meet the rest of the working group. They agreed to meet regularly for about an hour and a half every four to six weeks. Before each meeting, Peter asked them both to send him a short e-mail indicating the questions they wanted to work on in the meeting.

The first session set the scene for the project. It was important in this meeting to build a platform for later work, to inspire mutual trust and confidence in the work and to bring Peter up to speed with the clients' concerns and aspirations. The fact that he knew the sector well was of great help in this session.

The clients started talking about what they did **not** want: a voluminous report which would be put straight into a filing cabinet or into a wastepaper basket without being read.

So Peter asked a Future Perfect question, addressing Yvonne and Wolfgang at the same time. He asked them to imagine the three of them sitting together on a beautiful day in May 2006, after some months of very good work. What could they tell him about the results of their work, now that it was completed and done as well as they could have hoped? Peter asked them to speak in the present tense about what they had achieved.

Both described in detail their ideas of a future perfect. The main points were:

- There is a paper – clear, concise and very well structured – listing every relevant aspect of hospital design from patients' points of view.
- All the main stakeholders in the hospital sector are impressed by the long list of shortcomings featured in the paper.
- It is influential in future hospital planning with patients in mind.

Peter says:

> 'This gave us two perspectives on which we could work further. The first and most important goal was to write a paper by the deadline, summarising the material without missing out important aspects. The second was to express the guidelines for hospital planning in an impressive and compelling way which would really further the patients' interests.'

Peter set up a scale where 10 meant the Future Perfect they had described and 1 was the complete opposite of that. He asked Yvonne and Wolfgang what would be 'good enough' for them in the circumstances (to which they replied 8 or 9). He then asked them to scale where they were in their drafting the report with respect to both these perspectives. On both perspectives, they rated the current situation at about 3.

How good is 'good enough'?

The idea of 'good enough' when setting up scales is very useful. It's a good reminder that 10 is a direction and not a destination as well as a way of bringing a realistic acknowledgement of the real world in to the picture. It's very common in our experience for 'good enough' to be rather less than 10.

They rated the current situation at 3 because they had already achieved some progress toward their goals:

- They were optimistic that concentrating on patients' needs and publishing them could indeed influence the situation in hospitals. From examples in other countries (e.g. the development of standards for care in Scotland), they had learnt that this could be successful;
- They also knew that their working group trusted them completely. There was always a patient and understanding atmosphere in their meetings. Nobody had left the group because of frustration about the slow progress of work;
- By gathering all their material they had gained much more confidence in judging which aspects were more important for patients than others.

With skilful questioning, Yvonne and Wolfgang also recalled some useful counters from the past, when they had tackled similar tasks, for instance:

- When confronted with a large writing task, it had helped to start writing with the 'easy part';
- It was also helpful to let go preset patterns or models by first writing down what is in your mind and systemising the material later;
- Experience showed that people tend to be more impressed by ideas and recommendations with an inherent benefit for themselves than by evidence of their faults and shortcomings.

Find what worked in similar situations

Examining what was helpful in the past in tackling similar situations is an excellent way to start. It doesn't take long, but it can unearth all kinds of useful information and know-how.

By the end of this first session Yvonne and Wolfgang had the impression that they had already achieved a lot more than they had expected and there were some clear and simple first steps to do next. They decided, for instance, not to follow their original plan in which they wanted to start by building on a clear structure and formulating concise headlines for all the chapters. Instead they agreed that each of them would choose just one topic to start with. For each topic, they would write down the most important points on a single sheet of paper. They agreed to meet each other before the next session with Peter to compare what had emerged and what had worked for them.

Wolfgang says that he felt a great sense of relief in that first session:

'I gained confidence that we would be able to do the job. I found it astonishing that Peter didn't help us in the way I had expected. He didn't help at all with the content of the report, but with the process of writing it. I didn't realise this in the first session – that came later. In the first session, I was aware of his encouragement, but didn't know how he did it.'

Yvonne comments:

*'I thought he knew the answers and wanted us to find it for ourselves. The hospital expert had said that the task was easy; Peter gave the impression that he knew it **wasn't** easy, but it was possible! This gave us confidence in our own ability.'*

Acknowledge the challenge and ...

Acknowledging the challenge is an important part of platform building. Here, Peter shows that he is on the clients' side, well aware of how tough things are and yet confident that they will get through it.

Building on what works

The following five sessions always started by looking at the progress of the work. They focused on what had gone well and the parts of the draft paper that Yvonne and Wolfgang liked best. This gave them good examples on which to build. Yvonne says that Peter's use of questions rather than answers was helpful to them; Wolfgang adds that Peter supported them by concentrating on their successes. He says

> 'There was a critical point: we realised that in the material we had collected, everything was expressed as negative and bad – 'We don't like this' or 'So-and-so shouldn't happen'. Peter helped us to reverse this and express things in terms of what **was** wanted instead by showing us the Albert Model – a basic way to understand SF. I thought from my history as a student activist that 'To criticise is to struggle!', but I had learned through experience that criticism makes people defensive. Talking about what is wanted, not what isn't wanted, helps dialogue.'

Yvonne talks about the power of examples in discussions about what is wanted.

> 'There is a variety of things that people who say 'no-one speaks my language' might want. We heard things like 'I want a friend who speaks my language and German to be with me' and 'I want the hospital to provide a translator' and 'I want to learn German'. It's easier to create new things with examples like these which made everything more alive. People can connect with real examples.'
>
> 'And it's more fun!' she adds.

What's wanted is not the opposite of what's not wanted

Talking about what is wanted is more than just motivational. Saying what we don't want tells us very little about what we do want. It's a bit like going to the supermarket with a list of all the things we don't need this week. What is wanted and what is not wanted are not binary either/or opposites. In terms of the Albert model, they are on different axes.

Writing the paper

The paper developed gradually in both form and content. Writing became easier given a solid base to build upon. Yvonne and Wolfgang described this feature of emergence with a striking metaphor:

> *'It was like a crystal which needs a core around which it can constantly grow.'*

Starting with the easiest, the more guidelines were written down, the easier it became to find a systematic way of describing them. A system of nine chapters emerged with concise headings. They became clearer by formulating them as statements in the present tense, for instance 'We co-operate with patients' or 'Accessibility to the hospital is guaranteed for everyone.'

To make it as concrete as possible, these headings were followed by examples of good practice to show hospitals the kind of things they could do to meet patients' needs. For example, 'the hospital ensures on an organisational and personal level that the patients' needs are always listened to and borne in mind in making decisions about them'. And in the chapter about co-operation for example, 'the hospital's staff are trained to show an interest in the wishes and complaints of patients or their relatives and there are special people to whom patients can talk in confidence.'

During the report writing phase, there were two more meetings of the working group. Yvonne and Wolfgang found it much easier to prepare and facilitate these meetings with the confidence of achieving a well-structured paper in mind. The focus on what was wanted and the use of real examples from experience helped the discussions go smoothly.

Grow change like a crystal

The metaphor of the core around which the crystal grows is very striking. In this case Wolfgang and Yvonne used a useful SF technique to choose their core – start with the easiest! When things look challenging and there are many choices, this is one way to decide how to begin, and then to learn more about the process as it develops.

Results and outcome

The obvious and visible result of the process is a concise framework to aid hospital planning from the patients' perspective. It consists of a title page and index, a summary page and guidelines for using the document, followed by a page describing 15 guidelines and ending with a page with the names of all the people involved in the process. It was ready in time to be cross-checked by a third party before presenting it to the KGK on the due date.

The guidelines included things like accessibility, security, confidentiality, privacy, shared responsibility in decision making, communication, provision of information, respect – especially of the needs of specific groups like senior citizens, women and children and immigrants.

There was a lot of appreciation by the KGK for the concrete nature of the paper and for managing the working group. This was the first time progress had been made on the topic of the patients' perspectives and needs in hospitals.

What's next?

Meeting Yvonne and Wolfgang, Mark and Jenny were struck by their focus on the patients' interests and their determination to do all they can to represent their interests. They are starting to work with individual hospitals, drawing on the ideas of the staff themselves in the same way that Peter did with them. Hospitals in Germany work in a competitive environment and helping them to see things from the patients' perspective could be of great assistance both in helping patients in their choice of a suitable hospital for their needs and as a self evaluation tool for the hospitals themselves.

Their enthusiasm has spread all over Germany. Various institutions in other cities and counties, including Berlin, Stuttgart and Munich, have expressed interest in using this work as a basis for their own development.

Peter's Reflections

The long phase of gathering material was probably necessary. Gradually, the clients became acquainted with the topic and the way people think about it. For a while, the sheer amount of material they

had gathered was overwhelming and they felt they were stuck –
paralysed by the size of the task.

Peter says:

> 'As a consultant I had to decide how much I wanted to be involved in the
> clients' system. I chose to keep my activities as simple as possible by
> working exclusively with the two facilitators – and not with the working
> group. My expectation was that coaching Yvonne and Wolfgang would
> have positive effects not only on the desired result but also on the whole
> system – and it worked!
>
> Unsticking them was quite easy thanks to the questions asked in the
> beginning of our work together, for instance: What do you want to
> achieve? And how do you feel about achieving it? What is this about?'

The constant focus on the things that worked gave the clients the
confidence and discipline to carry on step by step. They became more
confident in formulating ideas and standards in a positive way. The
greatest relief happened when they abandoned their aspiration of
completeness. By listing examples of good practice they created a
paper that others could add to or update with more examples.

Peter was very struck by the difference it made to ask his clients to
write down their ideas, thoughts and experience between meetings.

> 'Now I think about asking more clients to write papers about their work.
> My guess is that the act of writing things down is an aid to learning for
> some clients. I first discovered this by asking clients to write a sentence
> or two about what they want before we meet. One responded by writing
> a whole report. This saved a lot of time at the beginning of the assign-
> ment. The platform is already partly built by the time we first meet as
> the written words give me a good starting point in discovering both their
> aspirations and resources.'

Writing the story changes the story

The idea of using writing exercises is one which could prove very fruitful. It connects with the idea of change as an act of changing language
by telling and retelling (and therefore changing) stories. The field of
narrative therapy is based on this idea, and leaders in that field such as
Michael White connect their work explicitly to a post-structural framework in similar ways to the Solutions Focus community.

Peter Röhrig is an SF consultant, trainer and coach in Cologne/Bonn (Germany). His formal education was as an economist and social scientist. A member of the SOLWorld steering group from the beginning, he is the inventor of SF quality development in Germany and has a passion for SF leadership training. His own leadership experience is in business and in his family. Peter loves singing and watching emotional movies.
Find out more about him at www.mehlem-institut.de

Dr. Peter Röhrig
Mehlem Institut für Qualitätsentwicklung: Gluckstr. 14, D 53115 Bonn
Consult Contor: Balthasarstr. 81, D 50670 Köln
Tel: +49–228–34 66 14
peter.roehrig@mehlem-institut.de
www.mehlem-institut.de
www.consultcontor.de

Chapter 7

Simple steps and Trojan mice

One manager's story of using SF in everyday work

Co-author: Mona Hojab

Organisation: Peabody Trust

Many of the cases in this book relate to specific projects and change initiatives. This is to be expected – Solutions Focus is a great way of handling organisational change and bringing people together to achieve it. This chapter is a little different. How can SF ideas be used by individuals in everyday situations to help make progress?

Here we will learn about a very personal journey by one person, in an organisation that initially knew nothing about SF ideas. This is a situation which many will recognise: how can one person use SF ideas without the support and help of those around them? One answer is to use the ideas to generate results rather than talk about them. This chapter shows how many different elements of SF practice can be used to keep things moving in challenging situations.

Mona Hojab and Peabody Trust

Mona Hojab is Head of Learning & Development at the Peabody Trust, one of London's leading housing associations. Its roots go back to 1862 when a donation from American merchant banker George Peabody started a charitable organisation to support and house the poor of the city. The organisation now provides social housing for over 50,000 people in 20,000 properties, and employs around 600 people.

Mona came to Peabody from the Industrial Society, where she had attended an initial two-day training in Solutions Focus applied to change management. She had then been involved with an initiative to apply SF to improve the way training was delivered as well as various internal processes including the performance review process, 360 feedback tool and client evaluation forms.

When she moved to Peabody Trust, as Head of Learning and Development she was responsible for devising and delivering learning and training interventions that would ensure that staff and managers were equipped to deal with current and future business challenges. The way she tackled the job and the results she obtained were informed by her experience of SF in action.

> *'It's about an attitude. Ten years ago I might have felt the need to make a big bang entrance, try to do something big and high profile to make a statement – a very non SF approach. But now I am able to do things differently. I didn't start off by trying to appear to have all the answers – I didn't. After all every case is different! I just got on with talking to people finding out what they were doing, starting to take small steps. I didn't say I would change the face of Learning and Development. But I did eventually have a big impact on Learning and Development through lots of those small steps.'*

Where to start?

One of Mona's first challenges was presented to her during her interview for the job. What do you do with managers who are cynical about training?

> *'I knew the textbook answer to this. I should have said 'You motivate them, work with them, bring them on board and so on'. However, I decided to respond truthfully. My response was very SF. I said that I wouldn't bother with them. I would find mangers who are already on board and are keen and I would work with them. Why waste your energy on the cynical managers when there are other managers who are interested and keen?*
>
> *I extended this idea into using my time with colleagues. I identified peers and colleagues who were positive, enthusiastic and doing well in their job and spent more time with them. I found out what they wanted from Learning and Development and helped them to get it.'*

This way of deciding where to focus effort and attention is a version of 'finding the customer for change'. In SF work a customer for change is defined as someone who:

- Wants something to be different, **AND**
- Is prepared to do something about it

Work with the green people

When you want to make progress, working with the people who want to see change is a good place to start. In a traffic-light inspired metaphor, we call this working with the green people – as opposed to the amber people (who are not sure yet but will probably join in) or the red people (who are definitely not keen). Things start to happen, and the resulting news of progress will encourage engagement by others.

One such example was the Policy team within the Trust.

'The Policy Team was very important in terms of setting resident policy and also very influential in that they were responsible for training all staff in how to apply those policies. They do a lot of interacting with the rest of the organisation as well as the residents. The manager asked for Train the Trainer training for her team. I offered them a two day workshop in accelerated learning methods and processes, which they accepted and enjoyed. The benefits of this simple piece of work was far reaching. On a personal level, it enabled me to create an important connection with a key team in a very informal and natural way. The fact that they worked with all areas of the Trust meant that they also became 'ambassadors' of the Learning and Development Service. On an organisational level they were able to deliver better training in a more compelling way for which they received a lot of feedback

This for me is such a SF way – a little step, easily reached, yet with so much impact.'

Trojan Mice

You will probably be familiar with the ancient story of the Trojan Horse. According to Virgil, the inhabitants of Troy were securely holed up inside the city walls, with the attacking Greeks held at bay outside. The siege had lasted ten years, with the Greeks trying all manner of ways to break into the city.

Finally the Greeks built a giant wooden horse, ostensibly as a gift and tribute to the besieged Trojans. They left the horse outside the city gates and left. Despite some initial misgivings the Trojans accepted this 'parting gift' and wheeled it into the city. That night Greek soldiers led by Odysseus climbed out from their hiding place inside the horse, opened the gates and let in their compatriots (who had been in hiding nearby). Needless to say, the Greeks were victorious.

Over the years this idea of a Trojan horse has come to mean something that is allowed in and then has large scale consequences. The latest variant is the Trojan type of computer virus, which appears harmless but has serious consequences when executed.

The idea of Trojan mice has appeared recently as a development of this basic idea. Placing a single big horse outside the city, although bold, is not a very reliable strategy. It takes a long time to build. It may be refused (as the Trojans nearly did). The soldiers inside may be discovered. And if any of these things happens, the entire strategy is ruined. This may be seen as analogous to a big managed change programme – it's a lot of effort, which may all be overturned in an instant.

The idea of Trojan mice is similar, but different. Rather than having one big horse, how about having lots of small mice. These look less significant, but any one of them may have a big impact if it gets through. In organisational terms, Trojan mice are small changes which are easily accepted by the organisation, but which may develop into large scale significance. Sometimes these may involve new connections between existing systems or practices, or small changes to build on things which already work.

Not all of these Trojan mice will 'get through' – that is, will bring about long term change. However, if they are well chosen and implemented it is likely that some will prove significant in the long term. Of course, it is impossible at the outset to say which will succeed and which will not. The thing to do is to set the mice running, keep an eye on them and encourage those which persist. Mona says:

'The idea of Trojan mice was a key working principle for me. I tend to treat every single interaction as a way of setting forth a Trojan mouse

who will support and sell what I'm trying to achieve. It never mattered how junior, senior, or high profile the person was, I always tried to treat that interaction as the most important thing for me and to make sure that a step was taken, no matter how small, to provide them with a good service. I didn't plan anything a long way in advance. Things seemed to evolve and develop in useful ways, which I was able to build and encourage with more small steps.

'Another advantage of thinking in terms of small steps is that, if something goes wrong, it was only a small thing. There is less at stake to start with, and the odd failure is accepted as just part of finding what works. It's very different to having a big step that doesn't work out.'

This idea of Trojan mice extended to people as well as actions.

'One of the individuals I had trained in accelerated learning processes then moved and started working in a different part of the organisation. It was then very interesting to see how the training she received impacted on her new role.'

Use small steps as Trojan mice

Not every small step will succeed. You may want to set several things running and see what happens – then build on the more successful. Treat small steps as experiments. The key thing is to notice which steps are having an impact, and not get too disappointed about some things which may come to nothing.

Simplifying – build on the good things

Mona found a lot of good things in place at Peabody. So that these things could be seen and used more clearly, she set about simplifying things by removing extraneous matters and helping people to focus more clearly on the important stuff.

'We had a complicated performance management process and competencies. There were different forms for different levels and different competencies for different roles. This system would have worked well in an organisation with a long history of performance management processes which was well versed in them. The Trust however was not at that stage and needed a system to reflect where the organisation and its

people are at. It's about thinking what does the organisation want and not what I want.'

Taking a positive focus has helped Mona in different ways:

'I started to look to build on the good that was already happening. I was always trying to find what worked and build on it in small steps. I found that I was then being invited to a lot of quite important meetings! People seemed to like having that perspective on what they were doing. I found that I was becoming much more influential as an individual than I had ever been in the past when I was less solutions focused. Being solutions focused helped me create a very positive vibe about myself and my work. I think people are attracted by that.'

Don't just notice what's working – talk about it

Next time you notice somebody acting effectively, consider letting them know. When someone else quietly comments on what you are doing that's working, it's very different from simply having your own view to consider.

Alongside this Mona felt herself being able to act in a very different way at work. Rather than want to be in control all the time she began to feel comfortable with taking small steps and seeing what happened.

'I developed a certain confidence in the SF approach. Small steps can and do make a difference, and I don't have to be in control all the time. This is not rocket science, but it's so powerful. I just do my job, but it's how I do my job that has made such a big difference.'

Future Perfect

Mona had learned about SF from Mark McKergow and Paul Jackson, and she enjoyed their use of Solutions Tools as pieces of technique. Mona says that she used these for herself in starting her new role.

'Future Perfect was very important for me. I knew what I wanted in general terms – I wanted the L&D team to be creative, leading edge,

professional, flexible and client-focused. I didn't want a department driven by policies and rules – being flexible was important. But it was another thing to do a Future Perfect on all this and start to think about 'How would I know tomorrow that this was starting to happen?'. That gave me something I could start to do right away.

'Then, when I started to do it I was able again to act on small things. I never felt the burden of having to be perfect right away; we always took small steps in the right direction. This is very poignant for me – I have not always been like this. I used to always think 'This is the way we should do it!' and then get upset when we didn't, or couldn't do it like that. It was such hard work trying to be clever and right all the time. I always tried to be a 10. Now if I think I am at 4, I wonder what I can do to get towards 5?'

Shift your paradigm with a small step

There is usually something comforting and motivating about thinking about the next small step up the scale. In this case Mona talks about the huge changes that can result from stopping thinking about change as all-or-nothing, and breaking it down into small steps. This shift can be radical and instantaneous.

Counters

Mona has used the SF idea of Counters – building on things that are already working – in many ways.

'I was asked to develop a Leadership programme. Ideally I would have loved to develop a five-day residential programme for all senior managers – but there is no way I'd ever be able to get them all together for such a length of time. Getting them together all in the same room for a reasonable amount of time was going to be a real challenge for me. I then tried to think of ways that I could engineer that. I took a an SF approach of asking myself 'when does that already happen?' and the answer was so obvious to me. 'We were already having full leadership team meetings (about twenty people), for one morning every two months. This seemed to work well – everyone showed up. So I asked if we could use the afternoons for short sessions about leadership, and that was the start of the Leadership Programme.'

Beware of theories

In SF work we have the idea of being wary of theories and explanations – particularly if they are not directly connected with progress. Steve de Shazer once wrote that theories were, at best, useless. They lead to explanations which are dubious and not connected to solutions – what is wanted. Mona is mindful of this all the time and will often steer people away from working with theories to working with real issues and to look for successful examples.

> 'One of the Action Learning Sets in our Management Development Programme was tasked with looking at how to improve our communications. It seemed that we had a silo culture – one where people communicate mainly vertically within their own departments rather than horizontally across departments. The Set came to me asking for good books or conferences on Silo cultures that would help inform their project.
>
> 'I suggested that they keep away from books and conferences because they will just give them theories about silo cultures and ideal solutions. We don't live in an ideal world and it seemed so much more Solutions Focused to tell the team to go and and find real organisations or teams that don't have a silo culture and examine what they're doing differently and learn from that. We came up with theatre companies (external) and our Community Regeneration group (internal). This is all so logical.'

Find where it's working – internally and externally

The SF principle of 'find what works' can extend far and wide. Here Mona is sensibly looking in different places for examples of the thing she is trying to do. This is very different from becoming an expert on the thing you don't want by reading books and attending conferences about it!

Things I could do myself

When Mona started to get to grips with her new role, she decided to focus not just on small things, but small things she could do for herself. Even more important was that the small things she could do herself would also be seen by and involve others.

'I started to use the Affirm idea as a tiny step on its own. I just started to publicise some successes to people – 'Did you know that last month our HR team delivered x courses?' , 'Did you know that last year we saved £x by delivering all our finance training internally', 'Did you know that last year the XYZ attended 95% of all training programmes that they'd booked on', that sort of thing, good news and successes really. I also started to let people know the situation, without commenting on it – 'Cancellations on courses have cost us £10,000 this month', 'last year 300 people didn't turn up on courses they'd booked on – this cost us £x.' without any further comment.

'One of the big issues we had in Learning and Development was people turning up late to courses. It somehow was OK to be late for training. So, a small step I took was to say that if people were more than 20 minutes late, they could not join the course and would have to come back another day. Setting the standard, this is what I expect. I was sending out the message that learning was an essential business activity and needed to be treated accordingly. As a result cancellations and lateness reduced. This all had a big impact, and it was something very small that I could do.

*'Another thing I did was to give people more choice/control over their learning. I strongly resisted making training mandatory. The programmes we always had trouble with were the mandatory ones. It's so simple ... . If people commit to training that they choose, then let's give them more choice'. Many of our courses are 'highly recommended', but it's up to people to look after their learning, act like adults and then behave like adults. People **can** turn up on time if they want to.'*

Work with the healthy adult within

Some approaches to change stress the importance of surfacing and working with one's 'inner wounded child'. In SF practice we take a similar view, but rather than finding a wounded child we prefer to unearth traces of a healthy adult. Giving people choices and trusting their judgement are two possible aspects of this.

Conclusion

Mona is still excited by the number of ways she has found of taking SF ideas and using them in small ways in her job. The Trust was short listed for an award from Housing Today magazine 'skills development'.

> *'We did not win the award, but that's not a problem. What I found very interesting was that we weren't even trying to get noticed or nominated. All I was trying to do was to find simple solutions for what's not working by building on what's working.*
>
> *'I have never had such good ratings as a trainer or been as influential as a manager as I am now. I think it's because I stopped trying to be influential, and let things happen for me. I have heard people say 'Oh, that's such a Mona way of doing things'. Most people seem to respond well to this. 'Just one thing we can do' is now a part of the language around here.'*

Mona's team has since been recognised with an award for high performance.

Mona Hojab is a Learning and Development specialist with senior operational management experience. She is also a practising coach and consultant. She has worked in a broad range of organisations and industry sectors.
mona.hojab@btopenworld.com

Chapter 8

Optimising the organisation

Restructuring at Freescale Semiconductor

Jenny Clarke and Mark McKergow

Organisation: Freescale Semiconductor

Reorganising a complex manufacturing operation is a complicated business fraught with difficulties. In this case, Chris McCann and his colleagues at Freescale Semiconductor used Solutions Focus ideas to tap into the organisation's know-how and creativity to keep the process simple and effective.

Freescale Semiconductor is a global leader in the design and manufacture of embedded semiconductors (chips) for wireless, networking, automotive, consumer and industrial markets. The company provides original equipment manufacturers with chips to help them drive advanced cell phones, manage Internet traffic and to help make vehicles safer and more energy efficient. Although you may never have heard of Freescale, you almost certainly use their products every day – in cell phones, AV equipment, white goods and cars. After more than 50 years as a part of Motorola, the company became a stand alone company in July 2004.

The competitiveness in the global semiconductor market means there is an ongoing challenge to drive continuous improvement in factory performance. Mark McKergow and Jenny Clarke had previously worked with the East Kilbride factory in the implementation phase of a cost-saving project, following McKinsey recommendations for standardised working practices throughout the company, based on analysis and best practice. This time, they were invited to help the factory to re-design its organisational structure in order to drive further performance improvements and to make full use of the talents and skills of the experienced workforce.

The factory in East Kilbride, part of Scotland's Silicon Glen, opened in 1969. It is one of seven Freescale Wafer Fabrication plants all over the world. It is an important employer in the area, with the majority of the highly skilled employees directly involved in manufacturing. One of the challenges is that the factory operates 24 hours a day 7 days a week with rotating shift and fixed dayshift communities. With the highly technical nature of semiconductor manufacturing, there is a large engineering support function which also operates 24 x 7 and on dayshift. For this very reason, a matrix is necessary and this was an opportunity to look at different ways of organising the resource.

Reorganising the structure

The Organisation Optimisation Team (OOT), led by Engineering Manager Chris McCann, was set up to devise an organisational structure which would help deliver the business objectives placed on the factory. Just as important were the 'soft' considerations about the ethos of the factory. The objectives were to:

- Enhance the sense of common purpose and team spirit
- Engage the staff in the process of change
- Develop individual and collective ownership and responsibility
- Develop new skills
- Recognise success
- Ensure good alignment of functional areas

The existing organisation

Machine operators and some engineering and technical staff worked on 12 hour shifts, supported by managerial and engineering staff working 5 days a week. This led to a complicated matrix of reporting lines, with different lines for day-to-day technical matters, special projects and traditional type line management. The complexity was compounded by the number of levels in the hierarchy: an operator working on shift at a machine looked up to a Group Leader, a Supervisor (working on rotating shifts and not often at work at the same time) and two levels of day-shift management above that. The operator would also come into contact with an engineering organisation which had a similar hierarchy and mixture of shift workers and day-shift personnel. It was further complicated by the rotating shift technical staff reporting to different management from dayshift technical staff. Was there an opportunity to simplify and provide clarity to roles and responsibilities within this complex structure? – this was the challenge set to the project team.

Data gathering workshop

Chris McCann recognised the importance of involving people from all parts of the factory in the project. This would improve both the quality of the outcome and the transparency of the change process. It would also create a coalition of change agents to help in deploying any subsequent change. This was an opportunity to directly engage a wide cross section of the workforce and model a new working climate.

Chris was keen to use SF ideas in engaging people in a positive and constructive way. He asked Mark and Jenny to design and facilitate workshops to discover more about the ways in which the various departments and groups in the factory saw the opportunities presented by a change in organisation. Two separate workshops were convened, each attended by a cross section of a dozen staff to give representatives of function, hierarchy and geography within the factory.

Benefits of change – for everyone involved

After the introductions and scene setting, the group listed the 'stakeholders' in the project – parties who would be affected by the outcome. These were identified as the operators; engineering staff – on shift and day workers; the supervisors; section managers; line managers; the top team at the factory; the top level management in the USA and Freescale customers. Working in three smaller groups, they then considered the benefits each of the stakeholders could gain from a better organisation. This is an important element of Platform Building, helping everyone see the point of the re-organisation exercise and the advantages that might stem from it for them and for others. This led to energetic conversation and was a good medium for exchanging views and gaining understanding of different perspectives.

Benefits of what's there already

Next, in randomised pairs, the group interviewed each other about what worked well – from their own perspectives – about the current organisation.

> – Which aspect of the organisation works best at the moment?
>   - What's good about it? What else? ... (more detail)
> – Which other aspects work well?
>   - What's good about it? What else? ... (more detail again)

This may seem a surprising step when change is in the air. However, it's important to build on what's there already, and this process offers ways to identify and retain what is already working. The output from this was captured on flip charts, and added to the sense of optimism and possibility – it was a good process for reminding people of what was already good about the organisation and to ensure that this was not compromised by the change process. Not surprisingly, however, the conversations were punctuated by lots of 'buts' – 'Yes, that's going well, but ... .'

This generated what Daniel Meier calls 'Hot Topics' – things we must get right. The conversation was energetic and co-operative rather than the moaning session it might have been had the question been 'What's wrong with the current organisation?' This is the value of careful platform building (benefits exercise) and the search for counters (what works well now?) and the affirms implicit in that search. The group identified the following Hot Topics

- Need for clarity in roles, expectations and reporting lines
- Authority/responsibility well-matched and well-understood
- Reduced points of contact – less time reporting and conveying and seeking information and more time doing the job
- Handovers – right time, right people, right information
- 'Big Daddy' information system so that everyone has access to the information they need, when they need it
- Shared understanding of priorities and clearer guidance about them
- People management implications of 400 people on fixed shifts with the rest rotating round them
- Shift autonomy/self sufficiency
- Training issues

> ## List 'things we must get right' rather than problem issues
>
> Phrasing the hot topics as 'things we must get right' offers the chance for people to raise problems, issues and concerns – but in a way which points them to state them in a positive way. The things we must get right are a much more focused list than the 'things we must not get wrong'.

Future Perfect

This proved a useful set-up for the Future Perfect. In this case, the participants were asked to 'suppose that you could wave a magic wand and all the topics you have identified are instantly resolved in the way that you would like them to be. What would 24 hours in the life of the factory be like, from your own point of view?' Everyone spent about 5 minutes pondering this question alone, and then formed two teams each with one representative from each stakeholder group to produce a story board showing the factory from midnight to midnight.

The storyboards showed snapshot pictures of key events during the day, with each individual team member appearing in at least one picture. This helps to keep the story very specific (as it involves these specific people, not just any old employees) and draws the people into the story they are developing. As well as jokey requests for bags of money, they included important details about who should meet, when and what information should be exchanged.

After lunch, the same two teams spent some time considering their storyboards and drawing out the implications and questions arising from their idealised pictures. Despite the fact that the magical transformation allowed them to think in an unrestricted way, the teams came up with highly compatible ideas in the Future Perfect storyboards.

> ## Two Future Perfects can be better than one
>
> In our experience, the fact that the two groups produced compatible Future Perfect descriptions is not unusual. It seems that in thinking about the details of what they would have in an unconstrained way, people can produce something on which they can agree. Additionally, the points of agreement are instantly clear and can be utilised straight away.

Developing different perspectives

Next, participants were paired so that everyone worked with someone from the same stakeholder group. Their task was to make posters addressing the following questions:

- How could things work from your point of view?
- Who would you communicate with on a typical day?
- What do you need from the people you interface with?
- What do you think they need from you?

The posters were arranged on the wall to form a 'Gallery walk'. Participants were free to spend about 10 minutes looking at the exhibits and then each pair introduced their own poster and responded to questions and comments from the others. This took about an hour and generated very valuable detail about interfaces, information flows and levels of authority and responsibility. The focus on interfaces and communication helped to develop a sense of how the organisation would organise itself, rather than simply looking at each group's activities in isolation. Again, notice that this is all about possibilities in the future – nothing to do with what is there already, what is wrong with the current situation, etc.

Organisations are their conversations, not just their people

The focus on interactions and communications, rather than individuals, is a key part of the Solutions Focus approach. The question is not so much 'what will I be doing' as 'how will I know what to be doing'? This links to the narrative idea of organisations as collections of conversations rather than collections of people.

Affirms and small steps

Finally, participants were invited to tell the group what had impressed them about their colleagues and what they were looking forward to as the project reached its conclusions. Many common threads emerged here: the workshop itself was energising and enjoyable; everyone was open-minded, thoughtful and honest; it was good to be involved in early thinking; there were many points of view and different interests but many shared concerns: everyone wanted to see the factory do well.

Chris McCann comments:

> 'The project team was really encouraged by these first workshops – particularly with the level of engagement and energy that the process generated. The variety of processes used allowed very detailed information to be gathered and open and lively debate in areas that would not surface in other brainstorm style processes previously used in the factory. This provided great insight and made the next stage of the change process much easier than it could have been.

> 'There was a great level of openness and willingness to share things. The process leads to this – you get it without even realising it. It allowed us to surface areas where there were potentially conflicting viewpoints, but it did it in a way that was non-threatening and constructive, and produced lots of detailed information on what people wanted which produced really good insights.

> 'And another thing – the workshop was fun and people enjoyed participating. Sometimes we do brainstorming and problem solving processes and it can get quite off-putting for the operators and supervisors. We really got the best out of the people. They even worked through their lunches without complaining!'

The revised structure

Chris McCann and his OOT team took the results of the two workshops and produced a proposed revised structure, which drew on the information gathered at the first workshops. Mark and Jenny also drew together their views on the topics raised in the workshops, providing an outsider's viewpoint.

The major changes from the previous organisation recognised the participants' ideas. They aimed at improved accountability and alignment by making technical management responsible for both the dayshift and rotating technical support roles. Dayshift engineering would now have the lead role here, aided by the introduction of a new post of Lead Technician working on shift as the primary interface between the production and the technical shift communities.

At this stage the project team combined the terrifically detailed output generated from the workshops with their more customary Digital Six Sigma methodology to evaluate possible organisational designs against a model proposed by the Hay Group in a paper entitled 'Designing Highly Accountable Organisations'. This led to a proposed structure and organisational model.

Next steps – testing and implementation workshops

The team wanted to present these proposals to the people involved in the workshops, with the aims of:

- Testing out the proposals with those who would be implementing them;
- Adjusting the proposed structure to improve it;
- Gathering support and momentum for the changes to come.

Chris McCann invited Mark and Jenny to run follow up workshops two months later. The workshops were structured into three sections:

- Presenting the new structure
- Working with the proposals
- Looking forward to implementing the structure

Once the new structure had been presented and questions of clarification answered, the participants were asked to imagine themselves working in the new organisation and, with colleagues in similar positions, to consider these questions:

- Take a few moments to think about the impact of the new arrangements:
  - How things will work well on a typical day
  - What will help you carry out your role better
  - How will you get the support you need and give support to colleagues
  - What advantages can you see?
  - What questions are there?

Then, working in mixed groups, they discussed the questions raised. How could things be made to work? What should happen in times of crisis or emergency? And so on. Issues were raised and options considered, all in a positive and constructive atmosphere.

To consolidate this work, the participants were asked to draw up the new structure for themselves, in a way which made the benefits of reorganisation clear. This both allowed the OOT team to be clear about the conclusions reached, and helped them to clarify the benefits and to think about how they could start to communicate them to colleagues outside the workshop.

Chris McCann: *'Not everyone would have come into the room agreeing that our proposal was the way to go. Presenting the new structure to the whole cross-sectional group meant that all could understand why it was being proposed this way, and all were able to accept the reasoning for it. The discussion in the first workshop showed a variety of viewpoints which everyone had heard, and so everyone was aware of the various views.'*

Looking forward to implementing the structure

Next, the group started to address the process of implementation with a Hot Topics process:

- In implementing the new structure, what are the things we must get right?

Having listed these, they turned to looking for counters about change in the East Kilbride plant. In groups, the participants considered their experience:

- Each think back to a time when a change was implemented in the factory (preferably successfully!)
- What helped it to go well then?

Chris sat in the front of the room in the role of a consultant who was about to tackle the change process. He asked the group questions about what they would advise him to do and which steps should be taken next, based on previous experience. The group provided answers for him, based on their thinking about past successful changes.

Chris says:

'This was a really useful part of the process for me. We had successfully ratified our ideas for a new structure, and this then formed the first steps towards a plan for implementation.'

Changing roles changes conversations

The setup for this activity seemed important – Mark and Jenny put Chris at the front in the role of someone who knew nothing and asked the group to share their advice. The 'role' part of this seems important – if Chris had simply asked for advice as himself, the group would have had to try to work out what he already knew, rather than just saying what they wanted to say.

Having collected ideas big and small from these positive experiences in the past, the group started to look forwards:

- How can we apply these previous good practices to the present change?
- What small steps would you like to see happening next?
  - For Chris and the team
  - For you as part of this group

In this way, the small steps were something that everyone was considering for themselves as part of the process. Spreading good words about the forthcoming changes was a key part of the desired result for the team, and Mark and Jenny built on this with the final process of the day:

- What are you going to tell people
  - About this meeting?
  - About the new organisation?
  - About what's going to happen next

The day finished with a lively 'cocktail party' exercise where people mingled and practised saying what they were going to say to each other and colleagues back at their workplace (and also heard their colleagues' ideas and views).

Practise and improve your stories

This kind of exercise, where people quickly try out saying the things they want to say, can work in a very interesting way. We have noticed that people change, adapt and improve their words – particularly if they are encouraged to. Seeing someone's reaction to your words in a fun and encouraging environment can be an excellent process for all concerned.

Chris McCann: *'The second workshop was useful for checking in and ratifying the work to date, and keeping the people involved in the process. We were able to turn an important corner in the overall process – from testing our ideas to see how they were received to generating an implementation plan.'*

Following these second workshops, Chris and his team revised and presented their proposals to the management team. These were accepted, and the new role of Lead Technician was put into place. Chris used SF ideas to implement the new role with those selected to carry it out – perhaps that's another story ...

Chris McCann: *'Looking back from here, my overall summary is that the change would not have been successful without the inclusion of the Solutions Focus processes. They were the key to unlocking the door, so that we could tap into the best experiences of the people and talents we had on the site. It's a technical environment and we use problem solving approaches every day. The SF approach gave us something different from the conventional approaches.'*

Reference

Daniel Meier (2005), Team Coaching with the SolutionCircle, Cheltenham: Solutions Books

M. Dalziel, S. De Voge, K. LeMaire (2004), Organizational Redesign in the Journal of Organizational Excellence, Vol. 23, Issue 4, pp. 59–66.

Mark McKergow and Jenny Clarke run the Centre for Solutions Focus at Work (sfwork). The Centre develops practical positive approaches to the everyday activity of work – including coaching, evaluation, project management, appraisal, strategic planning and more.

sf work
26 Christchurch Road, Chelteham, GL50 2PL, UK
+ 44 8453 707145
mark@sfwork.com
jenny@sfwork.com

Chapter 9

Solutions Focus tackles complexity

Finding a way forwards through the legal and regulatory jungle

Co-author: Kirsten Dierolf

Organisation: Bayer CropScience

It's one thing to know how to reach out effectively. It's quite a different thing to know what the goals should be. In this chapter, SF methods help a world leader in innovation to navigate a useful and sustainable path through scientific, technical and regulatory complexity.

Bayer CropScience is one of the world's leading innovative crop science companies, working in the areas of crop protection, non-agricultural pest control, seeds and plant biotechnology. Based in Monheim, Germany, the company has a global workforce of about 18,800 and annual sales of about €6 billion. It is represented in more than 120 countries.

The European Commission was drafting new legislation affecting the agro-chemical industry and the company had appointed a consulting company to help it make sure that its interests were taken into account in the drafting process. The consultants were very helpful in advising on the mechanics of stakeholder involvement – how and where to do it – but not so helpful in identifying the message that they wanted the European Commission to take on board.

Strategy and legislation

Hans Mattaar, the European Regulatory Strategy Manager, called Kirsten Dierolf to tell her about a difficult situation he was facing.

He had a team of international experts with very different fields of expertise: lawyers, marketing experts, scientific experts and regulatory affairs experts. Their task was to find proposals to put to the European Commission working on a Thematic Strategy on the Sustainable Use of Pesticides and on new legislation about bringing plant protection products to the market.

Of course, Hans welcomed a system that improved safety – to have a regulatory regime for the authorisation of plant protection products which protected man, animals and the environment. Moreover, he wanted to respond in a constructive, thoughtful way to the topic, resisting the more common knee-jerk responses from the industry – very technocratic, answering science with science. His focus was on what the legislation should want to achieve as far as Bayer and its sector of the industry were concerned. This required some different thinking and creativity using all the different competences in the team.

The team had already met a couple of times and although fruitful, it was very difficult to move forward given the high complexity of the issue: whenever there was a glimpse of a way forward in one corner, twenty 'yes, buts' raised their ugly heads in the other.

Hans had met Kirsten before, and heard about the Solutions Focus approach from her. The ideas made sense to him as he met problem focused thinking all the time. He was also concerned that his team members, with their academic and scientific backgrounds, often lost sight of the big picture. The idea of trying the approach appealed to him and so he called Kirsten: could Solutions Focus be helpful in such a situation?

Solutions Focused processes are applicable in so many fields because they are mostly about human interaction. Be it in business, in therapy, in conflict resolution, or team training, solutions focus is a good way of helping people change quickly and sustainably. However, in this case, they were only talking about a limited human relationship component. It was not that the team had difficulties amongst themselves or that they wanted to change their way of working together. Rather they needed to find a compelling message to influence the European Commission in drafting strategy and legislation about the use of pesticides and other plant protection products. This message needed to take into account the safety of plant protection products, the interests of Bayer CropScience and the plant protection industry in general and, of course the interests of the European regulatory bodies. Hans' team and the lobbying experts knew *how* to reach out, but were not so sure *what* messages they should be conveying.

Platform building

Before Kirsten started to work, she was extensively briefed about the issues at hand. She was sent an impressive stack of legal and technical documentation to read. She says:

> *'As a solutions focused practitioner, blessed with a beginner's mind and remembering that every case is different, I was wondering whether I should actually read all of the information which one could interpret as belonging to the problem and not to the solution. In this case, I decided against my long developed solutions focused intuition and read every-thing diligently. We also had half a day's briefing with the public affairs consultants and the customer to help me understand what exactly 'the problem' was.'*

It later turned out that this was a very useful thing to do. By talking about the problem and about the attempted solutions, she found the way into the language and grammar of the team and that was very helpful in two ways:

- *'It made joining the team and collaborating with them much easier: there was no irritation about 'why is she here' or 'she doesn't even know anything about our business, how can she help us?'*
- *'I could distinguish between when someone was talking about a way forward and when someone was engaging in less useful analy-sis of why something would not work. Given the highly technical and legal terminology, this would otherwise hardly have been possible to do.'*

This is an important point. Although Solutions Focus practitioners are not interested in problems for their own sake, it is important to listen to clients talking about them. It enhances the consultant's credibility (by learning the language, jargon and history) and it demonstrates that the consultant is listening with interest and concern. Of course, the consultant is listening – with interest and concern – for hints about what the client wants. Traces of this are usually there, hidden in all the details of problem talk. Kirsten says

'Whenever I have the feeling I don't know enough about the problem, I turn it into wondering about what they want.'

Solutions focused, not problem phobic

Just because Kirsten is solutions focused does not mean that she is problem phobic. It's important to listen carefully to the story of the problem for two reasons, neither of which is related to finding information about the problem to solve it. Firstly, it helps to join with the clients in the project. Secondly, there will be traces of a solution-narrative to be noticed and amplified later – hints about what's wanted, useful strengths, times when things are better and so on.

The Workshop

Kirsten had a day with the team. There were eight or nine people from different disciplines and from all over Europe (Spain, Germany, UK, Netherlands, Belgium).

She started with a short introduction to the approach using the analogy of the 'game of life' (see for example http://www.bitstorm. org/gameoflife). The computerised game consists of a collection of cells which, based on a few mathematical rules, can appear, survive or die in each succeeding time period. Depending on the initial conditions, the cells form various patterns throughout the course of the game. This is a complex yet non-complicated system governed by only a few rules and yet it is mathematically intractable – there is no quick way to work out how or when the system will settle into a stable configuration. The only way to find out is to let the system work itself through one step at a time.

Analysing the present cannot predict the future

The Game of Life shows the futility of trying to determine the future by analysing the present. If this is not possible in such an apparently simple system, why should we expect our complicated world to be different? All we can do is act now, see what happens and adjust accordingly. SF offers a way to choose how to act now, and to build on whatever useful change occurs.

If there is no short cut to predicting the fate of cellular automata following simple rules, what makes us think that we can predict the outcome of infinitely more complex human situations?

We may know how public affairs activities work – someone talks to someone else; some people are influential, some people know how to use this influence constructively .... But we cannot know in advance exactly what the outcome will be – we just have to wait and see!

This straightforward analogy convinced most team members that it would not help to keep analysing the problem in all its facets and that solutions focus methods could offer a way out.

People may or may not want to know the theory

In this case Kirsten found it useful to make explicit the futility of analysing the problem. In general this is not necessary, but in this environment and working with people accustomed to a technical and analytical method she found it useful.

Kirsten then led the team in a series of activities following the structure of an individual solution focused interview, based on the work of Daniel Meier (2005) and of Paul Z Jackson and Mark McKergow (2002)

Goals for the meeting
It is useful to start work of this kind by setting expectations for the day – and setting them high! Asking what people hope to achieve during a session is a great way to concentrate minds on the task in hand – and to head off any misunderstandings about the objectives from the beginning. Kirsten first invited the whole team to fast forward to the final feedback round at the end of the day and said 'It is now 15:30, ladies and gentlemen, we are finished with the session. Could you please give me a summary of what you have achieved?' Answers were 'to get new ideas', 'to start developing a 'product', 'some content', 'think outside the box' and 'follow a structured and creative process.' Most people were comfortable with this rather surprising beginning – some team members seemed not so used to it, but interactions were lively.

Stakeholder Outreach Goals

The team then broke into two working groups, one addressing the strategy document (Thematic Strategy on the Sustainable Use of Pesticides) and the other working on the new legislation governing bringing plant protection products to the market. Each group was asked to come up with specific, concrete desired outcomes from the industry's point of view and the viewpoint of the other relevant stakeholders.

The groups developed very interesting details of the goals. The group working on Thematic Strategy formulated a few goals such as 'minimising risks for health and environment and being recognised for the effort to do so', 'Avoiding illegal use of plant protection products', and 'reducing impact of plant protection products by innovation' and already linked these to goals of the European Authorities and other stakeholders. The group working on plant protection products formulated 'strict regulatory standards favoring innovative and safe products', 'being recognised as a provider of enabling technology for healthy crops', and a 'predictable, consistent regulatory process' and also already linked the goals to the respective other stakeholders.

Goals are not the Future Perfect

These goals are a useful part of building the platform. They are statements of what is wanted in the future. The other future aspect of SF practice – the Future Perfect – is different. In that process, people describe a world where the goals have been achieved with particular reference to the differences so created. Both have their places in skillful practice, and the distinction is well brought out here.

Scaling – where are you now?

The whole team was brought back together to exchange and enlarge on each other's work and then Kirsten asked where people thought they currently stood on a scale from 1 to 10, where 10 meant that they had found which content to push for and they knew how they would like the legislation to go and it was incorporated in the legislation and 1 meant the opposite. She drew a scale on a flip chart and invited individual members to put a sticky dot on what they thought the appropriate point on the scale was. The results were between 3 and 5.

Counter finding

There was no discussion of the actual numbers on the scale. The important thing was that everyone thought something of what they wanted was already incorporated in the drafts and the legislative process. This simple fact was a rich source of information. Working in pairs, the team worked questions like these:

- Describe recent successes with regard to finding what you want and communicating it to authorities
- What helped? What else?
- What is working well? What are the 'exceptions to the problem'
- Can you identify 'signposts to solutions'?

Their answers were noted on post-it notes, put onto a pin-board, and then the team grouped common ideas together. This raised the energy, enthusiasm and optimism and led Kirsten to ask the Miracle Question:

The Future Perfect

She asked the whole team to

'Just suppose .. that after we finish here today ... and you fight the traffic, hop on a plane and go home ... and do all the things you have to do this evening ... and finally go to bed ... and go to sleep. And while you're asleep, a miracle happens ... and all your problems concerning these issues are resolved, just like that. But the miracle happened in the middle of the night and you didn't see it happen. How would you know, when you woke up, that a miracle had happened?'

This led to a series of good, coherent ideas, which Kirsten captured on a flip chart. She then widened the scope of the miracle by bringing in other perspectives (the Commission, member states, the farmers who buy Bayer products and other stakeholders):

- *How would other stakeholders know that a miracle had happened?*
- *What would they see you doing that you are not doing now?*
- *What would they be doing?*

> ### *It's never too late to talk about the miracle*
>
> Kirsten has used the Future Perfect tool quite late in this process. Notice how she widens the picture to bring in other perspectives. The process expands the group's perspective in an interesting way.

Small Steps

To decide on some small steps in the right direction, Kirsten used the idea of scaling in another way. This time, she introduced a 'Scaling Walk'. She marked out a scale from 1 to 10 (10 being the miracle) in the room and asked the participants to stand at the appropriate point on the scale to show their perception of where the company was now. She encouraged some more counter-finding conversation at this point and then asked everyone to say they what they would notice if they were one step higher on the scale. This very quickly led to do-able, concrete action plans with responsible persons for each action. Examples were finding alliances in and outside the company or drafting a new and easier regulatory process.

These were recorded on a flip chart, with details of who was going to do what and when they would report. Contrary to normal experience, all the actions were completed to the agreed point before the follow-up meeting 4 weeks later. This meeting happened without Kirsten, as it was technical and needed no further support from her side. Kirsten says: *'It is my aim to make myself superfluous as quickly as possible.'*

> ### *What would one point higher look like?*
>
> Expanding on the description of 'one point higher' is a very useful tactic. The phrasing that Kirsten uses, to ask about what people would notice, is significant. This invites a description in which, rather like the Future Perfect, the people have not had to take action – they simply have to think about what they would notice was different. This usually acts as a helpful springboard to picking some small actions.

Feedback from the workshop

Six weeks after the first workshop, Felix Hirschburger of Resourcefulsearch interviewed Hans Mattaar to find out what had happened in the meantime and what – if anything – had been especially useful in how the workshop was run. The interview was arranged after the team's follow-up meeting because, in common with coaching and therapy sessions, the real change happens after meeting the consultant. In the follow-up interview, Hans said that immediately after the session he would have assessed the usefulness of the workshop at a 6 or 7 and was a bit disappointed with the outcome, but he was very happy with the next session and then rated the helpfulness of the original session at 8. He said

> 'When we looked back at the action points that we had taken from the meeting, it turned out that people had actually followed up on these action points. They had all done it, they were motivated to do something with it.'

He was surprised about the lag, but explained it by likening the process to turning the wheel on an oil tanker – it takes time to respond. The signs that things were moving were apparent in the second meeting where he detected a new approach to the project.

When asked what was most useful for the group, he replied that concentrating on the things that were already working helped the most:

> 'The most helpful element I thought was that part where people were forced to think about things that do work in the current system. ... We still have people from that group who in current meetings say: 'I know I should not say 'but'' So this approach apparently has lasted well with the group. It is a new mindset but it is difficult, especially in this business because there are certain areas where it is very hard to find anything that works.'

They also discovered what can and cannot be done in complex situations and found an efficient a way to deal adequately with complexity:

> 'Getting more insight into the fact that when you talk about highly complicated systems or processes, it is useless to try and attempt to analyse the entire causal relationships within that process. If you try to do that, you can only feel that you are in control of things if you over-

simplify the situation. ... You run the risk of losing too many elements from view. ... I now understand that it is really good to acknowledge that you cannot oversee the entire process for the next two or three years – to decide where you want to be in the absolute ideal situation and what would be necessary to ever get there. There is no point in trying to map out the entire route, because tomorrow there will be a change in some other legislation, or there will be a change in European government. You don't need to be a follower of the chaos theory to understand that any small change can throw the system that you so carefully thought out and that could be very frustrating. So just concentrate on the next few small steps in the right general direction. On the one hand keep your eyes on the goal at the horizon, and at the same time concentrate just on the next few steps you have to make rather than sitting there and wasting your time on planning the entire route which will change anyway.'

Stay out of 'ant country'

The idea of 'one eye on the horizon, the other on the ground in front' sums up an important element of SF practice. You can know what you want (the horizon) and what's next (the ground in front). The territory in between, memorably described as Ant Country by scientists Ian Stewart and Jack Cohen, is unknowable in detail in the same way as Game of Life. Attempting to foresee it in detail is to put energy and attention where it is least useful.

On a more personal level, Hans said

'One thing I personally learned from this is to not try and go too fast. I have a tendency to want to see the final position on the chessboard before I make the next move, so taking it a step at a time requires some effort. I am trying to learn to decide which direction I want to go, and try to keep the horizon AND the ground in mind. I used to rush to the goal and then miss the big hole in front of me! '

Later reflections

For the purposes of this book, we interviewed Hans Mattaar nine months after the workshop. From this later perspective, his reflections are interesting. He comments that the workshop was a small part of a very long process which is still ongoing. It is not easy to keep this kind of approach alive throughout the project, or to train younger regulatory staff to accept that there is more than just science in doing a good job! However, the approach is still bearing fruit:

> *'I hear people saying things that I would not have heard five years ago. Not just because of a single workshop, but this gave me a handle on things as to how to tackle it. I am trying to cascade this down into the company. The way that a different kind of approach is brought to a group is crucial to how they pick it up and use it. This worked quite well with this group. For me it was very important to have the next meeting to fully appreciate the change it had brought to the group.'*

These comments are very interesting. As Solutions Focus practitioners we notice that asking for client feedback serves more purposes than a client satisfaction survey aimed at improving our own practice. It is a positive intervention in itself, serving as a reflective tool for the client and helping to

- reinforce learning
- aid reflection and review
- give rise to more insights
- create ripples through the client's organisation

SF as a practice of simplifying

This case shows the strength of the Solutions Focus approach in messy and complex situations. One way of describing SF practice is as a way of simplifying a situation in a novel way. The usual way of dealing with complexity is to compare what's happening with some kind of schema or model, which in turn suggests what to do. The medical process of diagnosis and many models of personality and business work in this way. The SF approach is not to fit the situation to a pre-determined framework but instead to reduce complexity by overlooking aspects which do not relate to what is wanted. This usually means paying less attention to the problem and its cause.

Kirsten has insightful comments about the theoretical underpinning to solutions focus work. This is her perspective on the topic:

> *'Ludwig Wittgenstein wrote 'The belief in causality is the superstition.'*

Things happen after one another, but that does not necessarily mean that they are bound by laws of cause and effect. If you focus your awareness on a very simple context (thereby blocking out everything else that is happening), cause and effect seem to make sense: I prick a balloon with a pin – it explodes. The closer you look, however, the more complicated it gets. (For example what made me prick the balloon, why this balloon, who blew it up in the first place, etc etc). Choosing the scope of the problem influences how we think we can deal with it and how difficult or solvable it appears to us.

'Interpersonal relations or psychological problems are very complex if you take into account the whole context. They become so complex and interrelated that even an analysis seems impossible, let alone a solution. This is, in my view, why traditional psychology resorted to classification and diagnoses – simplifications and generalisations to make manageable the unmanageable. This also explains why effective solution finding processes in complex situations are very similar to one another independent of the diagnosis attributed to the problem.

'Solutions Focus makes it possible to start a change in the desired direction without having to reduce the complexity of the context. Knowing that the context and the influencing parameters are ever changing in human relations, Solutions Focused practitioners do not attempt to plan the whole change process from start to finish in detailed steps – it is simply not possible.

'The problems that Solutions Focus had already proven to work with and the more technical or political problem my client was facing had one thing in common: their complexity and ever changing context. And this is what led us to believe that a solutions focused process would be a good means to help the group to move ahead.'

Taken at this level, the possible use of SF ideas in areas other than issues of human interaction becomes clearer. It seems these could be a promising area for testing and research.

References

Robert Axelrod (2001): Harnessing Complexity, Basic Books
Steve De Shazer (1994): Words Were Originally Magic, Norton
James Kennedy (2001): Swarm Intelligence, Morgan Kaufman
Daniel Meier (2005): Team Coaching with the Solutioncircle, Solutions Books

Paul Z Jackson and Mark McKergow (2002): The Solutions Focus, Nicholas Brealey Publishing

Gunther Schmidt (2004): Liebesaffairen zwischen Problem und Lösung, Carl Auer

Ian Stewart and Jack Cohen (1997): Figments of Reality, Cambridge University Press

Ludwig Wittgenstein (1973): Philosophical Investigations, Prentice Hall

Websites:
Game of life — http://www.bitstorm.org/gameoflife/
Conversations with: Louis Cauffman, Jenny Clarke, Felix Hirschburger, Steve de Shazer, Insoo Kim Berg, Mark McKergow

Kirsten Dierolf M.A., founder of SolutionsAcademy, is an organisational developer, trainer, and coach working mainly for the banking, pharmaceutical, information technology and automotive industries. She teaches at two German business schools and is the proud mother of 3 sons and 2 tomcats. Her interests are her work, archery, juggling, classical music, and literature.

Kirsten Dierolf, SolutionsAcademy
Kalbacherstr. 7, 61352 Bad Homburg
info@solutionsacademy.com
www.solutionsacademy.com

Chapter 10

Creating a future when facing redundancy

Solutions Focused outplacement at Lufthansa Cargo

Co-author: Monika Houck

Organisation: Lufthansa Cargo AG

This case tells the story of an internal manager – not an outside consultant – and how she applied SF principles in offering outplacement as part of a major cost cutting exercise.

Lufthansa Cargo, part of the German Lufthansa airline group, faced a very competitive market in 2004. Overcapacity in the market had made the competition for business even more pressing, and customers were in a strong position in their search for high quality service at keen prices. This simple fact persuaded the company to concentrate on its core business – flying cargo from one airport to the other. This is a highly competitive, overcrowded business and so the company also embarked on a major cost cutting exercise, stopping some projects, and reducing the number of employees.

Projects were cut and 10% of the 4800–strong workforce lost their jobs. In the headquarters the position was even more severe: of the 800 employees, 300 were now redundant. For human and business reasons, Lufthansa wanted to achieve this manpower reduction in a responsible way, one that maintained the trust of remaining staff in their employer as well as doing the right thing by those being asked to leave.

How to cut 300 jobs?

This was the first time in the history of Lufthansa that people in headquarters functions were affected by job losses: more than 30% of the people working in strategy, marketing, financial control and information technology lost their jobs. Many of those people had been with the company for many years. Most were highly-qualified, with very specific expertise in the airline industry. More than 60% were team-leaders or project managers; more than 20% were more than 50 years old; over 40% had worked for more than 15 years in Lufthansa.

Those who lost their jobs had many questions:

- Was it the right decision to reduce headcount?
- Why me – my record is a good one?
- How do I find a new position – as my qualification is very specific?

The predominant feelings were disappointment, anger with the company and uncertainty about the future. Those who 'survived' the cuts were also concerned to see how the company dealt with the situation. Morale was low throughout the organisation. One manager commented:

'After the cuts were announced, the place was chaotic. The whole marketing department suddenly disappeared. The entire management team was changed. I had the feeling everyone was suddenly very busy focusing on themselves.'

It was important to Lufthansa Cargo to take some responsibility for the longer-term future of its employees by offering them a professional coaching programme, to be known as 'CreateFuture'. This would prove the company's good faith as an employer. It would also have business benefits by demonstrating new ways of investing in people. Incoming HR Director Oliver Kaden says:

'People were due some respect – many had worked for us for a long time, and others had joined recently in the expectation of a developing career. We were determined to offer them help in finding new positions, as well as a platform for sharing their emotions and concerns. In addition, time was pressing and we also had to move forwards with our new business. So everything had to come together quickly.'

Lufthansa Cargo decided early on that it would not lay off anyone in this situation but would find temporary assignments for them until the end of 2006. By then, it was expected that everyone would have found alternative jobs, within Lufthansa or outside.

'CreateFuture' – the programme

Seeking the right person to lead this important programme, Oliver Kaden asked Lufthansa Cargo Global key account manager Monika Houck to put something together. In addition to over 20 years experience in Lufthansa Cargo, Monika was an experienced coach and had been involved with career and outplacement coaching internally and externally. She had enjoyed applying a solutions focused approach to her work, based on training in systemic coaching with Ulrich Clement and Peter W. Gester, and also used constellation and psychodrama methods from time to time.

Monika decided to call the programme CreateFuture. It was offered to everyone who lost his or her job because of the company restructuring. Solutions Focused ideas were to be very important in the programme: building on the strengths, expertise and potential of everyone who decided to take part.

As programme manager, Monika was also responsible for the choice of external company, project management, timings, results and quality management. She was particularly keen to ensure the quality of the coaches.

How the programme was developed

HR and the board of Lufthansa Cargo worked together to set up the programme, working step by step:

- Analysing experiences and lessons learned within other companies;
- Evaluating potential partners as specialists for personnel development;
- Designing a programme appropriate to the Lufthansa situation and requirements.

Analysis of other companies' experience

Monika interviewed several companies in similar circumstances, for example German banks, a pharmaceutical company and an automotive company. The aims were to learn from others what worked and what didn't for them and to seek recommendations for external consultants. This is an example of active counter-finding, with the added bonus of giving confidence to senior managers in the proposed route.

Who else has succeeded in doing this?

This is an excellent and very simple example of using Solutions Focused thinking in a broad sense. Who else has succeeded in doing what we are trying to do? What helped them? This information is not to provide all the answers, but to give some ideas and confidence to add to the existing internal know-how.

The following lessons learned were important in the creation of the Lufthansa Cargo programme:

- communication is key – the objectives and value of the programme have to be understood
- participation must be voluntary
- confidentiality: time is needed to establish trust in the programme and the individual coaches – at first, coaches are seen as part of the plot to get rid of the workers
- the decision to take part in external job development must be anonymous
- the external provider has to be first class and offer a network of job opportunities
- there must be continuity

Evaluate potential partners as specialists for personnel development

Six potential partners were assessed. The main criteria for the final decision were:

- Expertise – evaluated by the proposals, profiles and references
- Scope of the offer – consultation, workshops, internet tools and data bases
- Access to job markets – type and number of offered job opportunities

- Creativity – openness to design a customised approach
- Willingness to cooperate – openness for a joint concept
- Price – appropriate pricing in relation to offered services.

The evaluation was done jointly and led to a clear choice of a partner – Lee Hecht Harrison. They were an experienced outplacement company, familiar with SF practice and well-used to the concept of building on strengths. Monika was particularly interested in how LHH chose their coaches; she was keen to discover how much strength in depth they could provide. Some other companies had been keen for her to meet one or two of their coaches, who invariably turned out to be experienced and capable – but how could she be sure of the quality of the coaches lower down the batting order?

LHH's way of selecting coaches was based around the importance of a positive attitude towards clients. The coach had to be able to build confidence in people, not just by coaching but also by deploying good managerial qualities, the idea being to support people to do things for themselves.

Design an appropriate programme
CreateFuture had two objectives: to encourage and build up self-confidence and at the same time deliver professional expertise on how to find a job successfully in a difficult economic situation.

The first element 'Discover oneself' was seen as a journey of discovery of one's individual identity, creativity, and potential, expertise and experience. The second element, 'Discover opportunities', was more outward looking. This element was designed to help people build up a network of people, inside and outside the company, and to become aware of alternative opportunities for development. The main tools within this process were one-to-one coaching and teamwork.

How the programme was implemented

The programme started with initial two-day workshops describing the programme and introducing participants to the coaches. The workshops were offered without demanding any future commitment; this was simply an opportunity to let people know what was on offer. Participants would choose a project for themselves, be it looking for another job within the company or outside, and work on this, in confidence, with the aid of a coach. They were offered a choice of an external coach from LHH, or an internal coach from a small team selected and managed by Monika.

Go slowly to go fast

The element of choice seems to us to be a good example of 'going slowly to go fast' in the early stages. There were several choices for the participants – to join in or not, to look internally or externally, to have a coach or not, and whether the coach should be internal or external. The project's aim of reconnecting people with their skills and confidence is supported by giving and respecting choice.

Participants were encouraged to see themselves as the masters of their destiny, working for a future that they wanted for themselves. For many participants, this was the first time they had met others in the same situation – and often team work and intense networking started immediately. Market research specialist Mario Perz remembers the impact of the first workshop:

'I had only joined Lufthansa Cargo about six months previously, and it was to be a case of Last In First Out! This shook my self-confidence very badly. I really did not know what I might do, or even if I could do a decent job for anyone any longer. The workshop was the first light at the end of the tunnel. It was a very important moment for me – I discovered that there were many people in the same situation, and we were all able to start right away. A few of us from my workshop continued to meet throughout the programme, which was also a great support.'

At the end of the introductory workshops, everyone was asked to decide whether he or she wanted to be part of the CreateFuture programme. More than 90% joined. Those who didn't were either close to retirement or had already found another post. Having started the programme, participants were allowed to spend up to 50% of their working time working on building a new professional position and career. In the end people took an average of about six months to find a new position.

Individual coaching

Everyone joining the programme could decide when to join. They were all offered five coaching sessions with Lee Hecht Harrison. For many of them, it was essential to talk to an expert who was not part of the company – their neutrality was seen as valuable.

About 20% of the participants chose internal coaches from the very beginning. Monika says there were three reasons for doing so:

- People who wanted to reposition themselves in Lufthansa thought that an internal coach would have more views and better contacts on how to do this
- Ethics – if I lost my job because of cost constraints, it doesn't seem right to spend money outside the company when we already have the expertise inside it
- Personal contacts – some people knew one of the coaches, and wanted that person to work with them.

All the internal coaches were HR professionals and certified coaches, working in training, personnel development or change management for many years. They had all trained as systemic coaches. Monika supervised them during the programme, using a Solution Focused format described below.

After the first five individual coaching sessions, participants reviewed the situation with Monika, then chose how to proceed: with an internal coach or as part of the network supported by the experts of the FutureLab.

The FutureLab was set up as a key place for the project in a suite of rooms in a special area at Lufthansa Cargo. Monika had told senior management to steer clear of the area. Staffed by two HR people the FutureLab was used for workshops and coaching, a source of news, new books and articles, and as a confidential place to work. There were phones and computers which the participants could use confidentially. This was an important place – somewhere for people to meet and work in pleasant surroundings.

The two staff played an important role in administering the programme – organising workshops, coaching dates, researching opportunities, helping people write specific CVs and letters, talking to LHH and keeping the FutureLab well stocked and ready. For Monika, the FutureLab was a very important communications centre – she could quickly get updates about what was happening.

Building up self-confidence

Imagine the situation of a 48 year old Lufhansa employee, with two children to support, who has been with the company for more than

20 years enjoying a successful career working as an IT-specialist responsible for specific flight plan programmes.

The first normal human reaction may be frustration and anger with the people he blames for getting the company into this situation: 'they have still got their jobs but I lost mine even though I always did a good job.' Or perhaps he gets depressed. Either way, his confidence in his ability to do a good job is tempered by doubt: 'will anybody employ me with my experience and qualifications?'

In these circumstances, it is vital to the success of the project to regain self-confidence and trust. The main tool to achieve this is to identify one's capabilities and potential.

Having offered the time and opportunity to openly talk about the situation, the coach's first question asks for individual objective within the coaching process. 'What do you personally want to achieve, for yourself?' The question helps to turn the focus of the attention away from the situation, the company and the management to oneself. Sometimes people, feeling depressed or aggressive towards the company, replied simply 'I don't know'. Few people were relaxed to start with. It often took time to gently engage them in doing something.

The useful meanings of 'I don't know'

Again, the idea of going slowly to go fast at the beginning shows up here. It can take some time for people to decide to engage, and trying to force the issue may well be counterproductive in the longer run. Here it seems that the people who replied 'I don't know' may have simply meant 'I haven't got around to thinking about that yet'. It probably doesn't mean 'I want you to tell me'.

The coaching process aims:

- to overcome negative feelings by a positive view of one's life;
- to start self-reflection and identification of values and interests;
- to become aware of who you are;
- to learn to communicate well, briefly and precisely – so that an outsider gets quickly an idea on 'who you are'.

A very important part of the coaching process is the identification of the specific competences that can be useful in looking for a new job – by building a personal profile.

Building a personal profile

The team of coaches, including Lee Hecht Harrison – many of them highly skilled and experienced in recruiting and developing people – pooled their own experience about what convinces decision makers that someone is the right person for the job. Their joint answer was that authenticity is key. When recruiting staff, people are impressed by someone who is genuine in what they want and clear about what they are able to do.

Much of the coaching work was to help participants get a clear picture of their aspirations and competences. Given a clear compelling picture, it is not difficult to communicate it to others.

Some questions proved to be helpful in the analysis of the competence profiles from the very beginning.

1. What was your best business experience within the last few years?
2. How did you achieve this?
3. What are the capabilities you used?

Question number one turns attention from the present situation to the past, in order to create a realistic and positive view of the future. The detailed analysis of past achievements changes the perspective of the coachee – he looks at himself with the eyes of an outsider – and starts to discover important strengths and capabilities.

The question 'how did you do this?' turns the coachee's attention to his own contribution and leads to a very specific, positive picture.

So the conclusion with the third question helps to create a competence profile that is realistic and convincing at the same time.

Mario Perz remembers the impact of this process in helping him to become more active in making progress:

'I was astonished at the number of things I had managed to forget about myself. At the beginning of the programme it seemed as if I had nothing to offer at all, but as we went on I found more and more previous events which could help me. For example in my previous job as a head of department I had been coaching others, helping to organise themselves and making presentations. All of these showed useful sides *of my character. I had also forgotten what it was like to really be a useful member of a team – and during the programme this came back to me.'*

Monika found that this kind of approach also allows further development of people's ideas about their strengths and achievements – for example by working in groups, listening to people's achievements and then by asking their colleagues to guess at the kind of strengths that might have helped.

Learning by rearranging what we know

This reminds us of Ludwig Wittgenstein's idea of 'learning by rearranging what we know.' By examining the small details of a positive and relevant experience certain aspects become clearer, even though nothing 'new' is taught and nothing has really changed ... or has it?

Team coaching – and networking

As well as the one-to-one coaching, participants were encouraged to work with colleagues in similar situations. From the very beginning three types of team events were offered by the FutureLab:

- Workshops in self-marketing techniques including video trainings.
- Workshops describing different market segments of interest as potential new employers
- Networking workshops that focused on building a support network, getting different perspectives of oneself and exchanging experiences

Other events included working breakfasts and networking events. Elements of improvisation were used very successfully within these workshops (Jackson, P. 2003). For example, one word stories and musical chairs, everyone who took a shower this morning gets up and moves, everyone who has been dancing last week. This helped participants to open up with each other and helped create common bonds between them. Peter Szabó ran a Solutionsurfing workshop for everyone in Lufthansa Cargo – in support of the process and the general mood of positive change management.

Supervision

The team of internal coaches met regularly for intervision using a version of the Solution Focused Reflecting Team methodology (Norman et al, 2005). This format is used by a group of coaches to apply their collected wisdom to difficult cases. The version used by Monika takes around half an hour per case:

Phase	Activity	Guidelines
Present 3′	Person presenting a case explains the situation	Only the person presenting the case talks
Clarify 10′	The team clarifies the situation: **a) regarding the facts** What? When? Who? How? Ask open questions and avoid asking 'why' **b) about the objective** How do you want it to be different? What would be the impact of the change? etc **c) on working sign-posts** What has been tried already and made some sort of a positive difference? What was useful? etc	The members of the team ask just one question each. Answers are only given by the person presenting the case. There might be a follow-up question. Everyone stays quiet until it is his/her turn.
Encourage 5′	Members of the team say what impressed them most on the person presenting the case and his/her behaviour in the given situation. Similar and appropriate compliments are allowed.	Members of the team speak in a random sequence. The person presenting the case stays quiet and just listens.
Reflect 5′	The members of the team express their thoughts related to the situation in terms of an open exchange of ideas. Statements may build on previous statements.	Members of the team speak in turn, making just one observation at a time. The person presenting the case stays quiet (if the statements are based continuously on a non useful misunderstanding, the person presenting the case may say so once)

Phase	Activity	Guidelines
Close 2'	The person presenting the case responds briefly to the reflections of the team: What was most useful? What might be applied?	Only the person presenting the case talks.

Monika discovered that this process ran well when:

– Someone is nominated to monitor the flow of the process and (if necessary) point out the guidelines so that everyone uses them.
– At the beginning and after each phase, the progress of the person presenting the case can be put on a scale where 1 means 'I don't have a clue how to continue with the coachee' and 10 means 'I have full trust in the client and myself to deal with the situation'.

Supervision with the coaches was held every two weeks initially, and then every four weeks. Using this appreciative way of building on the coach's individual strengths proved to be very useful. The creativity and the energy of the team were used to reinforce and complement existing coaching skills. From time to time, when it was thought desirable, an external supervisor was invited in.

> ### Scale on confidence in knowing what to do
>
> We like the variation in this version of the SF Reflecting Team method of adding a scale at the beginning and end of the process. Monika's choice of scale seems well-judged; the issue here is the coach's confidence in moving forward with the client, not the client's progress per se.

Coaching quality

Monika was very keen to ensure that the external coaching was of suitably high quality. There are various ways of doing this. Some organisations are keen to embark on hefty certification processes. Monika preferred a simpler and more interactional approach, using a systematic analysis of feedback from the participants. Participants were asked

• Did you achieve what you wanted?
• What do you appreciate about your coach?

- Would you recommend him or her for others, and if so, for which client groups?

The advantages of this approach are that the practice of the coach in their most recent work is under scrutiny – not whatever work they may have done to earn a certificate years ago. It also encourages coaches to be very focused on what their individual clients want, and offers the opportunity for the context of the coaching to be taken into account.

Feedback by appreciation and recommendation

This simple version of feedback is very useful. It avoids the absolute question of 'is this a good coach' and instead focused on the more useful and positive 'what are appropriate contexts for this person to coach'. It also focuses squarely on the client's achievements – surely a key indicator of the skill of the coach!

Monika worked with the individual coaches (on individual issues) and Lee Hecht Harrison for programme-wide issues. In cases where there had been problems, she phoned them, and gave them the opportunity to say how things had gone, then they worked out what to do.

What the programme achieved

By September 2006, all 480 of the participants had found a new position. In March that year, participants were interviewed anonymously about the programme: all of them said they would participate again. The greatest benefits of the programme from their point of view were the opportunity for self-reflection, the individual coaching and the networking opportunities.

The results of the programme are convincing:

- Self-confidence was built up
- The participants took responsibility for their own future
- More than 90% found a new position within 6 months and everyone had a job by September 2006
- Lufthansa Cargo regained the trust of its employees to a high degree.

Mario Perz reflects on his experience of the programme and says.

'The best thing was that I became absolutely confident of my ability to find another position – internal or external. In the end I became very interview-savvy and was really enjoying the process of meeting new employers, and their interest in my past achievements further under-lined what I had to offer in the future. In the end I found a position within Lufthansa which lets me use my market research background. Looking back, it has been an experience I would not like to have missed – I have learned a lot and made many new friends.'

His colleagues agreed:

'It helped a lot – especially the contact with the external consultants. I learned a lot within the workshops, lectures and by the many personal talks I had.'

'During CreateFuture I re-discovered my strengths and weaknesses. And I found the motivation to fight for my own interests.'

'Suddenly you start to think about yourself. Until then you were just a part of the puzzle – and now there was the opportunity to look across borders, discover new and exciting possibilities. CreateFuture is an excellent programme – a model for other companies.'

Monika says

'The solution focused approach was key to success within CreateFuture – to gain trust in one's own capabilities, values and interests again and to act accordingly.'

She sees the following factors as key to the project's success:

- Each participant received a personal letter from the board and had a conversation with his or her own line manager. In addition, the intranet had information, interviews and success stories etc.
- Participation in the programme was voluntary. Neverthe-less, more than 95% of the people involved decided to take part. Choice was probably a very important element in this high take-up rate.
- Confidentiality was ensured by separating the programme from HR and from the line managers
- Participation in the external job development is anonymous for Lufthansa Cargo

- Continuity was assured by providing a special place and team of experts – the 'FutureLab'

HR Director Oliver Kaden says

'The programme has gone very fast – indeed it finished six months earlier than we planned. I am very happy with what has been achieved – the participants had a platform for going forwards together in a professional way. We have also gained a lot in the eyes of the works council and unions, who have supported us at every stage. Even our customers have been impressed with the way we have acted, and the whole of the Lufthansa group has benefited from this project. Even though this was not a fun time for us, it has been a good experience.'

References

Paul Z Jackson, Mark McKergow: The Solutions Focus, Nicholas Brealey Publishing, London (2002)

Paul Z Jackson: 58 $1/2$ Ways to Improvise in Training, Crown House Publishing (2003)

Harry Norman, Micheal Hjerth and Tim Pidsley, Solution Focused Reflecting Teams in Action, in Mark McKergow and Jenny Clarke (eds) Positive Approaches to Change, SolutionsBooks, 2005.

Peter Szabó/Daniel Meier – www.weiterbildungsforum.com, Basel

Monika Houck is manager, trainer and coach with extensive leadership experience in HR, customer development, marketing, logistics and information technology.

Address: Monika Houck, Kapellenstr.7A, D 65193 Wiesbaden, Germany
Tel +49 171 194 6911, E-mail: Monika.Houck@dlh.de
Webpage: www.monikahouck.de

Chapter 11

Getting a team working together

Establishing more effective ways of working for a senior team

Co-authors: Peter Szabó and Daniel Meier

Organisation: EB Zurich

In this case study about team coaching, we see how two coaches provided the initial support for a new team of managers keen to find rules and procedures that everyone would follow. By focusing on the Future Perfect, they found a higher level desire to work well together, allowing them to overlook the more contentious issue of rules and procedures.

The management team of EB Zurich, a large institute for further education in Switzerland had just been through two extremely intensive years. They had to deal with a merger between two different schools, and the management team had grown from five to seven and then finally nine people.

In order to implement this change successfully, the management team hired the coaches Peter Szabó and Daniel Meier to work with them. In the initial conversation with Peter and Daniel, the managing director and his closest co-worker reported communication difficulties in the management team:

- Agreed procedures were not implemented
- Agenda items at the management team meeting were not well enough prepared
- Endless discussions ensued
- It was difficult to make decisions.

In short, they wanted to establish clear rules for working with each other – and they wanted these rules to be followed!

In this first conversation, the coaches listened very carefully and asked questions about the desired future:

'If this team coaching measure turns out to be successful, what will be different afterwards?'

'Who will be the first to notice a change – and what will they notice?'

Peter and Daniel let us eavesdrop on them talking about the situation

Peter: *What the two managers just described sounds very difficult and there does not seem to be much hope. I don't really know where we could start here.*

Daniel: *Yeah, you are right. But I am also amazed at the fact that they are asking for help so early. This does indicate a broad perspective and real interest in the issue. In many other teams, the external coach is only called in when things are so bad that the team can't work together any more.*

Peter: *OK. Do you think one initial day plus a half day follow up will be long enough for the coaching?*

Daniel: *I hope so. I am more concerned about how we are going to deal with the goal that they mentioned: 'Establishing clear rules for working together.' It bothers me a bit because I don't think that these rules and regulations are very helpful in general. But I don't see any alternatives at this point.*

Peter: *I was thinking along the same lines. It would be really nice if we could work on increasing choices rather than on strict rules. So, we would open up choices that support their common goal of working together better.*

Daniel: *Yes, definitely. That would also be more fun. First look at what has been working already and then open up new possibilities.*

What difference will the goals make?

This is an interesting conversation which suggests that the coaches didn't much like the clients' goals! However, as we see later, Peter and Daniel have a neat way of responding to stated goals by asking something like 'and what difference will that make?' This can lead to higher level goals – for example 'working together better'.

The first day of the workshop

On the first day of the workshop, the team and both coaches met just outside Zürich, at the edge of the forest with a view of the city.

At the beginning the coaches asked the members of the teams to introduce themselves briefly. They were asked to say which characteristics of their colleagues they valued in their work together. This already set a nice platform for mutual appreciation within the team and surfaced first hints on what behaviour was considered useful. The next step was to clarify the expectations and goals for the workshop.

After that, the coaches took a long strip of masking tape and taped it onto the floor across the whole room. They asked the members of the management team to position themselves on the tape:

'One end means that all your problems and questions concerning the way you work together are solved satisfactorily. If you put yourself at 10, your work would be so outstanding that it could be video-taped and distributed widely as an example of 'best practice'. And on the opposite end of the scale, at the other end of the masking tape, we have number 1: the absolute opposite of that, so that you could hardly bear to work with your colleagues for two more days. Where on this scale are you now?'

After the individual managers had positioned themselves on the scale (between 3 and 6), they were asked to work in small groups. The task was to have a close look and identify what was already going well in the way they worked together, allowing them to say they were higher than 1 on the scale. The participants were invited to look for small things, events, or experiences that were already pointing into the desired direction.

In small groups, the participants were then asked to develop common rules for working together in future on the basis of these findings. During this exercise, the groups discovered valuable clues pointing to what was already working well. For example, they noticed that they collaborated effectively and without tension when they were in small groups. They also found concrete hints for an efficient and appreciative facilitation of the management team meeting and realised what the structure of the agenda for their meetings could look like.

It was only when the three groups presented their 'rules of management' that they had developed that the first intensive discussions broke out. Some suggestions were diametrically opposed to others, and it seemed that these three sets of ideas could never ever be collated or integrated. One suggestion was based on consensus, another aimed at delegating to committees which would then decide with a single majority, and the third group wanted to install individual small cells which divide the work. The realisation of these differences took out a lot of the enthusiasm and the team went to lunch.

Let's listen to the coaches talking among themselves at lunchtime

Peter: *How can we possibly be helpful so that they can find a solution together?*

Daniel: *I don't see a way at the moment either. Maybe they simply need more time?*

Peter: *How do you manage to stay so calm and relaxed when they start debating so intensively? It is all about problems, there are no perspectives. We lost control of the conversation and I was afraid that we would lose control completely.*

Daniel: *I simply assume that there will be something useful in it for them. And honestly, I'm waiting for them to get tired of the discussion. This would be the right moment to start asking questions again. And additionally – if we believe in the ability of the team to organise themselves just a bit, then we know that these nine people must have the capacity to fight and then draw something constructive out of it.*

Peter: *You think that we sometimes just need more time until a whole team recognises a wave that is worth surfing on? You are probably right, but it is often so difficult to wait and to keep trusting the competencies of the people involved.*

Daniel: *Yes, that is not easy for me either. And they didn't seem to be getting tired. I think what also helped me to stay calm was that I did not understand much of what they were discussing. I could concentrate very well on understanding nothing and then asking a few targeted questions.*

Peter: *It was useful that you asked them 'what do you want instead' every once in a while. 'What would it have to be like so that you could work well in this management team.'*

Daniel: *How about dropping the issue of the rules and regulation for the moment and continuing with the Future Perfect? First develop a practical, action-oriented vision of the future and then later have the rules and regulations reflect that vision?*

Peter: *Sounds reasonable, although I am afraid that the Future Perfect will again produce infinite various ideas. Actually, they wanted to take back the rules and regulations into their usual management team meetings.*

Pick a route that looks fruitful

If one route seems to be a blind alley, approach things from a different direction. Here, Peter and Daniel decide to look at the Future Perfect and then – perhaps – work out what rules and regulations might help get there. We sometimes call this back casting – building and expanding on the Future Perfect to look at what else must be happening to sustain it.

Visiting the Future Perfect

The team agreed to drop the issue of rules for the time being and to work on a vision for the future together. First, they developed the 'future perfect' individually and then went out for a walk with a partner. After an hour or so, the whole group reconvened.

Christa was the first to speak up. 'Felix and I realised that our visions are very similar. When it is really going well in the 'future perfect', we are looking forward to the meeting. The paper work is short and concise, summarised to capture the essentials. We also have the opportunity to add other topics to the agenda ourselves.'

The coaches then asked the following questions:

- Imagine you are really looking forward to the session, what would be the other consequences?
- Are there any other ideas about what the future should look like?
- If we dropped by in a couple of months, how would we as coaches know that your trust in each other has increased and you are comfortable giving positive and negative feedback?
- If you knew each other better, what would be different then?

(This last question was suggested by the group. They felt like victims being thrown together by fate, with little in common and no desire to get to know each other better.)

This generated a very constructive sequence with a lot of energy. The participants then reflected in pairs about what they could do themselves to take small steps into the direction of the future perfect. 'What can each and every one do in our daily life to support the process constructively?' At the end of this sequence, there was a choice of 20 different concrete alternatives for action nicely written out on postcards and put on the floor. There were cards like 'discuss informally before bringing into the meeting' or 'prepare alternative options when asking for a team decision'. The participants proudly presented their ideas on what they might do different individually in the future.

Back to the coaches talking among themselves

Peter: *Hey, now this was a classic example of opening choices. Did you notice how the individual participants suddenly showed energy and were amazed at how improved working together can consist of many small building-blocks?*

Daniel: *Yes, I am also very impressed with the careful way the team dealt with this process. However, we have not finished this rules and regulations thing. We are running out of time.*

Peter: *And we haven't introduced the practical communication tools that we promised. What do you think, what do we want to give them to take home, scaling maybe?*

Daniel: *Exactly. They could spend the last five minutes at the end of each meeting scaling their communication and thus keep the process going. A short phase of focusing their awareness on where they are now and what has worked already?*

Peter: *We could demonstrate this at the end, right here. And then we could ask them to take away the flipcharts with the rules and regulations and continue working on them.*

Daniel: *What do you think about just asking them what should happen with the flipcharts. If we don't know what to do with them, maybe they do?*

Peter: *That's a great idea – taking seriously the client as expert. Yes indeed!*

Sparklers

The question of what to do with the rules and regulations flipchart caused another heated half-hour discussion. The team finally agreed to postpone the discussion to the next workshop. Just before the end, Peter had a suggestion. He said: 'I brought a tool with me for you. It is called 'sparkler'! As if by magic, he produced a pack of sparklers from his bag. 'I will hand out one sparkler to each of you. We'll conduct a small, secret experiment with them. Every time you notice that a colleague acted a little bit like you would like him her or to do you secretly place a sparkler (or a picture of a sparkler!) on his or her desk. Take care that nobody sees you and don't talk about it to the person. Who 'sparkled' whom and for what will stay a secret until our next meeting. If you get a sparkler yourself, of course, you can continue to 'sparkle''.

Two weeks later, a team member wrote an e-mail saying: 'Thanks again for this team workshop. The situation is more relaxed now. The sparklers have definitely contributed to this.' Only one person did not get a sparkler. He raised this topic at a team meeting, stating his disappointment and asking what he should do. He was flooded with sparklers soon afterwards.

Create conversations about positive change

The purpose of the sparklers here is as a mechanism to create conversations about positive change. Such conversations can be difficult without some kind of 'excuse' or prop to help them. Perhaps birthday cards serve a similar purpose in everyday life?

Coaches talking among themselves

Daniel: *What in the world made you think of the sparklers?*

Peter: *You asked me to bring some Christmas material when we called last night so I just saw some leftover sparklers and brought them along. And then while they were presenting their ideas I suddenly had the idea of how to use them. I thought it might help them to continue to focus on small successes and support them in their everyday life. Small changes in behaviour disappear quickly if they are not noticed and appreciated.*

Daniel: *On the one hand everyone is showing a certain awareness of the things that they perceive as changes – whether the other person has really changed something or not. On the other hand, everybody who receives a sparkler on their desk will ask him or herself what exactly they got it for. What he or she did that already points in the Future Perfect direction. And thus the focus of awareness remains on the desired changes.*

The second team workshop

The management team met the two coaches for a half-day follow-up four weeks later. The team (in groups of three) was given the task of noting what had changed for the better in the last few weeks. What happened next in the plenary can really be called a 'sparkling moment'. By persistently and consistently asking what was better and what else, Peter and Daniel created a space that the nine members of the management team used to find out exactly which developments had taken place, however inconspicuous. They discovered more and more important details. At the end of the round, the participants were even comparing themselves to successful sport teams.

It was then time to revisit the three forms of rules and regulations suggested in the previous workshop. The individual groups were very well prepared for the presentation of their work and the advantages of each one were discussed.

The full group recognised the similarities and differences in the ideas. Occasionally, very different views and positions flared up – expressed more clearly than before. The discussion, however, stayed factual. The nine managers selected a few of their members to form a group to be responsible for the rules and regulations and work on a compromise. One participant said:

> '*But something tells me that something has been set in motion. We have not come to an agreement yet, but we don't have to agree at this point. We have started to fight constructively and this is an essential difference to what used to happen before.*'

Final round

Daniel started the final round by asking 'On a scale of 1 to 10, 10 being the future perfect and 1 being the absolute opposite of that, where are you now at this point?' Everybody now was two or four points higher on the scale than they had been at the beginning of the first workshop.

The last quarter of an hour was used to answer the following: 'What can you all do (together or individually) to maintain this improved number on the scale?'

> ## *Build confidence about sustaining change*
>
> We like this question – asking about sustaining change, not just more progress. Of course, these actions may well lead to further positive change too.

Marlise Leinauer leads the department responsible for training the trainers, and is part of the management team. She says:

'The workshop helped us to find out that we could work better in small groups and reinforced that way of working together. We became aware of this as a result of the workshop and could build on it – we became more efficient in the way we worked. This was an important step for us in working to bring together the different managers from the two schools.'

Peter and Daniel's reflections

'Once again, we were amazed by the way that re-focusing people's atten-tion on what works changes their reality. We were really concerned towards the end of the first day, when they started arguing about the 'rules of management' again – we thought we'd lost it. But the sparklers idea, which came to us from nowhere, intrigued people and restored the sense of appreciation and enthusiasm. And it led to the astonishing improvements we saw in the second session.'

> ## *The art of being wise is the art of knowing what to overlook*
>
> We are fond of quoting William James who said *'The art of being wise is the art of knowing what to overlook.'* In this case, Peter and Daniel demonstrate their wisdom in overlooking the contentious issue of rules and regulations by seeing them as just a means to an end – the end being better collaboration. By creating a better climate, the team are able to deal with their differences more constructively, knowing that their aspirations are similar.

The eight elements of the 'SolutionCircle'

The 'SolutionCircle' tool was developed by Daniel Meier from the work of Steve de Shazer and Insoo Kim Berg. It consists of the following eight steps. They help tackle complex conflict situations in teams and enable them to use their energy for the sustainable development. Although presented in order here, the eight steps can be adapted to the situation.

1) Preparing the Ground

The first step serves to build trust in the coach and to agree on what is needed so that every one can participate fully. The coach creates the structure and the framework for the workshop, co-ordinates the procedure and roles and poses questions. The participants are responsible for the content and for developing solutions.

2) Expectations and Goals

The aim of this step is to define the criteria for success for the session. Which goals need to be met and which expectations fulfilled so that a participation in the workshop seems worthwhile? Here are some helpful questions that the coach might ask:

- What should happen in this workshop so that it is worthwhile for the participants to be there?
- What should be different after the workshop than before?
- How will you notice that you have reached your goal?

3) Hot Topics

In this step, we determine the 'hot topics', the things which need to be improved.

4) Highlights

The participants look for situations in which the problem or conflict occurred less or did not occur at all. They find out which competencies and skills enabled them to do this. The following questions might be used:

- What happened in the last weeks that seemed like a highlight as far as the problem is concerned?
- What exactly was different?
- What helped you to react in this way?
- What did you contribute to the fact that your colleague was able to react this way?

5) Future Perfect – developing an image of the solution
In the future perfect, the team develops a very precise picture of a future in which the problems are solved. Questions the coach might ask include:

- If the team developed exactly how we want it to – where would it stand in two years?
- What exactly would you be doing differently?
- What would others say about the team then?

6) Scaling Dance – what is already working well?
The individual members of the team assess the current situation in order to find out what has already worked in the past. Questions include:

- Imagine a scale of 1 to 10. Where are you now regarding the topic if 10 means the ideal state and 1 the absolute opposite?
- How did you manage to get to this point? What is the difference between 1 and this point?
- If you think about your highlights from step 5, where were they on the same scale? What is the difference here?
- What did you contribute personally so that you are on X on the scale?

7) Steps
In this step, the team decides on concrete measures that they can implement in the near future – preferably the following day.

8) Personal Mission
The coach gives an observation or action task to focus the awareness on certain aspects of the implementation. It is important to stay aware of what is starting to change for the better.

For more details and many practical tips on using SF ideas with teams, see Daniel's book Team Coaching with the SolutionCircle (SolutionsBooks, 2005)

Peter Szabó is a Master Certified Coach and a Doctor of Law. After 15 years in corporate HR management he has specialised in brief coaching. In his coaching practice he works with both individual and corporate clients on business and life coaching issues. He teaches coaching at several post-graduate university programmes throughout Europe. His latest publication is Brief Coaching for Lasting Solutions with Insoo Kim Berg (WW.Norton Publishers, 2005).

Daniel Meier originally trained as a teacher. He continued his education in Pedagogy, Adult Education and Management (WWZ University of Basel). Since 2001 he has been coaching managers, teams and organisations in a solution focused way during complex development processes. He is the author of Team Coaching with the SolutionCircle (Solutionbooks, 2005).

Daniel and Peter founded the international Brief-Coach training institute Solutionsurfers®, based in Switzerland. Daniel is the Director of the German speaking part of this association (www.weiterbildungsforum.ch), Peter leads the international Brief Coach training programme.

peter.szabo@solutionsurfers.com
daniel.meier@solutionsurfers.com
www.solutionsurfers.com

Chapter 12

Listening and letting go

Transforming a training department

Mark McKergow

Organisation: Chelsea Building Society

Solutions Focus is becoming known as an excellent approach for coaching, team development and organisational change. So how does it fare in different organisational settings? In this chapter we discover how SF helped the training department of a major financial institution – in more ways than we or they had thought possible.

The sixth largest building society in the United Kingdom, the Chelsea Building Society (www.thechelsea.co.uk), was established in London in 1875 – thirty years before the famous football team of the same name. The Society now has over 450,000 savers and 145,000 borrowers and assets of over £11bn. The organisation is a mutual – it is owned by its members rather than shareholders. This ethos of cooperation is important to the Society, which faces some considerably bigger aggressive competitors in the marketplace.

Chelsea relocated its headquarters from London to Cheltenham, Gloucestershire, in 1975 and now has a total staff of around one thousand people. About two thirds of these work at headquarters, the remainder in the 34 branches spread across the south of England.

Jeff Farish heads up the Training and Development department, with Mark Higgins as Training Manager. Both Mark and Jeff served in the Royal Air Force earlier in their careers, and come across as both level-headed and forward thinking. At the time we came into contact with Chelsea, Mark was looking for a way to continue to develop his group of eight trainers and support staff.

The group were already using some accelerated learning techniques and had a good reputation within the organisation for providing lively and productive learning events. Mark was looking for something to take their work up another notch. He knew Mark McKergow as a proponent of the latest in learning methodologies: he had delivered a successful seminar for the RAF on using music in learning some years previously, and moreover was living just down the road! Mark read up on Solutions Focus, and agreed with Jeff to look at introducing it to the rest of the team. At this stage none of them had any clue about the far-reaching impact that the SF approach would have on the department and the entire organisation.

The workshop

In May 2004 Mark McKergow and Paul Z Jackson delivered a two-day introduction to SF ideas based on their book The Solutions Focus. This focused strongly on the six solutions tools which have featured throughout this book, as well as taking a brief look at the desirability and usefulness of simplicity and the six SIMPLE principles. The workshop led up to coaching-type conversations between the participants, who seemed to enjoy the experience as well as helping each other find ways forward with their work.

At the end of the two days each participant picked out a quote or saying from the range of wall posters in the room, and told the group why they liked it and what it meant. Then the group went back to their work. Everyone had enjoyed the event, and Mark McKergow and Chelsea's Mark Higgins were eager to see how these experienced trainers might put their new knowledge into practice.

The impact – in training

When Mark got in touch with Chelsea Building Society some months later, he was delighted to be told that they had found many ways to use the Solutions Tools. And not just in training events, but also in many of the group's other activities. Mark listened open-mouthed as the list of applications grew longer and longer. Here are some of the trainers' stories:

Leadership and Sales training

Tom had found scaling a simple way to engage people. In the modules about feedback, he said that putting a number on the scale gives a context and sense of honesty to the conversation. Giving the feedback simply in words is, paradoxically, sometimes rather hard – putting a number on it it gives a context to the conversation and gives a sense of honesty.

> ## *Put a number on it*
>
> Put a number on it – we find again and again that the way numbers work brings this sense of concrete specifics to conversations. As long as the scale is a relevant one, everyone can agree that five is better than four. Then adding descriptions to these points can help explore the situation further.

Presentation Skills training

Wendy had started to use the scaling tool to bring learners' attention onto whatever they were already doing well in presentations. She found that this built confidence and started the course in a very good way. A Future Perfect element helped people to visit a great presentation they were giving. She then used an SF approach to feedback with the learners, always placing great importance on what had gone well. She stressed the importance of small steps in making progress.

Induction training, Health and Safety

Gareth used to dwell on what people were doing wrong in leaving hazards in the office. He had rebuilt the training to focus on what is a perfect office – one which was a safe as possible? He then asked people to go and identify what they had that fitted that, and how they could improve. He too had found scaling a good way to focus people's attention during this process.

Writing simply

Jeff picked up on the simple language elements of Solutions Focus and changed his writing style for greater impact. He had become even clearer about how simple words engage people, and had started to tell people about the power of '$5 words' – small, simple everyday words, and how these could be worth more than the abstract complexities of $5,000 words.

Use the power of $5 words

This aspect of simple language is a key part of Solutions Focused practice. It's interesting that Jeff, the senior manager, was the one to mention the power of the small word. Sometimes the length (and fog factor) of words seems to increase in proportion to people's seniority. Just using the power of $5 words can build change in your organisation.

Team building

Zoe had reformed her team building workshops to start with 'what's going well'. She then drew out a long list of counters – examples of useful change happening already which the team could use to move forwards together. She then moved on to a 'team Future Perfect' activity, where the team spent some time thinking about how it would be in a perfect world when they were working surprisingly well together.

Sales management team event

Mark had found the team wanting to talk about all their problems and generally moan. He listened and then proposed a Future Perfect activity, again with the team describing a miraculously good day at work. 'In 15 minutes we were there!' he says. The team began seeking and finding things to help them on the way – a positive and productive process.

Sales training

Tom had begun to start the course by asking the participants how they were using the system already (finding counters) and quickly building a good picture of broadly good practice. He then asked the participants to suppose they were selling mortgages to everyone, and notice what would be different in their work.

Gareth has also been using scaling during these courses. He asks people at the start of the course where they would like to be at the end. They describe it. Then he defines this as 10 on the scale, and asks them to rate their current position (taking care to define 0 in such a way that allows everyone to be at least 1 on the scale). They then discuss how come they are that high. Everyone places a sticker on a scale chart on the wall. At regular intervals during the week-long training Gareth asks the participants to revise the position of their sticker, and to reflect on what would take them the next step up the scale. Gareth says:

'This is a great way of having the participants decide for themselves what would make a next step. Often they say 'more practice' – and then we do some more practice. It's much easier than me telling them they need more practice. Sometimes they say it's time to go home – and then we do just that. There is also a degree of good-humoured conversation among the participants about people's positions on the scale. I find people saying things like 'You MUST be higher than that ... I saw you do well in the last exercise' and so on ... it's all in good fun, and it brings the subject of performance to the fore in a nice way.'

If you're working too hard, slow down

Passing over responsibility for moving higher on the scale is a splendid way of the trainer working less hard and gently helping the participants to work harder. We like to bear in mind the maxim that 'you shouldn't be working harder than your client' – at least not over a sustained period. If things start to get difficult, it's often because the trainer is working too hard and not engaging the others.

Wider impacts

As well as these changes to the training events themselves, the Chelsea team had also started to use SF ideas in their other work:

Developing learning

Training Needs Analysis is a key part of the role of any training department. Head of Staff Development Jeff Farish has found that using platform building and Future Perfect is great way to start this process.

'It's amazing', says Jeff. 'You ask people about what they really want, and then tell them to suppose that they suddenly and expectedly got it. What would be the tiny signs? The answer is often a long pause ...

followed by them telling you that they'll think about it. When they come back with some answers, you're off to a flying start. This is a really big advantage in getting this kind of process underway.'

e-learning

Gareth has included an SF framework in e-learning modules. In one example he leads people through training about the organisation's clear desk policy in the following way:

1. What remains on your desk at the end of the working day (tick boxes, for example computer, phone, photo of kids, paperwork, reading materials, pen tidy etc)
2. As far as you can remember, what do you think should be left on your desk at the end of the working day? (Write list).
3. With that in mind, how would you rate your desk for tidiness on a scale from 1–10, where 10 is computer and phone only, and 1 is 'looks like a bomb has hit it'. (Click number)
4. So you rate yourself a (N). What are you doing already at the end of the day to get this rating? (Type in what you are doing)
5. What else are you doing? (Type in more things)
6. So, you are already doing these things (they are listed). What small step can you now take to move yourself a little nearer to 10? (Type in small step)
7. Summary: You rated your desk as (N). You are already doing (list). To move yourself a step closer to 10, you will (small step)
8. Click to print out the summary. Well done you have committed to taking one small step towards complying with the policy. Check back in a week or two to move up another step.

What else?

This may be the first time we've been asked 'what else' by a computer! In SF practice this simple question is used often, to pile up counters and draw out long lists of things that are working. It's well worth using to help people think very carefully about their situations, and produce new ideas.

Facilitation

Mark Higgins has been using SF as a framework for team development. He has enjoyed the process, and has found that he can not only use the tools and techniques to help teams, he has also revised his own style of facilitation.

'I used to feel under great pressure to come up with ideas for the teams to try, and to help them fix their problems. Now I find a lot of benefit when I listen and let go – stop trying desperately to find a way forward and instead use the process to help the team listen to their own words and stories, and come up with their own ideas.

'What strikes me is the versatility of the model. For example, thinking about a team development day ... I might get them to create a Future Perfect picture with lots of blue sky thinking and creativity. On the other hand, I might look first at what is already going well and look for lots of examples where things have gone well. In fact, I recently ran a team event where we just focused on what was going well and what were the next steps. Then, the things that followed on from those next steps just happened naturally, without any need for further intervention.

'So the process is very robust – you don't always need to do a Future Perfect. Just looking at where we are now and how have we done what we have done lets people know that they are part of something much more special than they had realised before. One group then decided to seek feedback from the business, using a couple of the SF tools. They went to find out how the business saw them, and what they valued. They were pleasantly surprised with the results, and they came back to build on this ... then we did a Future Perfect, which was very productive.

'You can do interesting things with small actions too. On a team day a few weeks ago – each person took on a single next step, all aligned and moving things forwards. They agreed about how they would like to be seen, how they would like to operate. In general we have tried reducing the number of actions which come out of team days – in the old days people used to have a ton of actions and action plans, none of which came to much. We have even tried reducing it to ONE action – the most important next step. However, it's not necessary to do that all the time!

'To sum up, we have rarely used the all the tools together. In each area there are such valuable questions – they generate very valuable information and motivation, which you can then incorporate into your next moves.'

> ## *Choose your tools to fit the job*
>
> Solutions Focus is a very forgiving approach. As you get more accustomed to using it, you will find yourself better able, as Mark Higgins is, to choose a useful tool or question, use it well, and then put it down and choose another tool. Experienced SF practitioners don't choose their tools in advance, they turn up with a complete toolbox, size up the situation and THEN choose the tool to fit.

Running the Team

The Training team's internal planning and strategy sessions have also been touched by the SF approach. People still come with moans about things that have not gone well, but there comes a moment when the discussion is shifted around to developing a clear picture of what's wanted. This leads to a shift of the attention and onto more helpful matters, and the meetings get more productive and constructive.

Tom uses SF in working with his team of sales trainers on enhancing course content and for their own personal development:

> *'The scale of 1–10 where are you now, what are you doing better, what next small step would add value to the course ... This gives a nice structure to our conversations, and also it's always helping to move forward. Previously we didn't have a good and simple way to know we were going towards some useful actions.'*

Mark finds the focus on simplicity a valuable asset:

> *'We use the SIMPLE principles (from The Solutions Focus book) as a key guideline in what we do – it's pinned up next to my my desk, Jeff has a copy in view too. People use it all the time. For example, we are working on competences right now, and we are trying to simplify things. Lots of consultants offer very complicated versions, with lots of boxes and definitions. We are trying to think it through for ourselves and keep it simple, and that's helping our confidence as well as our creativity.*
>
> *'I have also noticed that in our team sessions people often start by saying what they want (looking for support), discussing what we have already, and then looking for next steps to move forwards. It gives a clarity to a frustration or a challenge to talk about it and enlist others in this way. It demuddles the situation – the conversation has a richer tone to it through this process.'*

Jeff adds:

'This language is also very non-confrontational – it's very forward looking, constructive, wanting to make progress. It really helps to focus other people as well ... getting people to look at small actions is particularly helpful.'

Simplify by clarifying, not by knowing

Ludwig Wittgenstein writes in his book Philosophical Investigations that the aim of philosophy is to 'battle against the bewitchment of our intelligence by means of language'. The role of the philosopher is to de-muddle linguistic and grammatical confusions. One way to look at SF practice in a broad sense is to see it as about helping people by de-muddling, rather than as helping them by knowing the answer.

Strategic Impact

In the two years since the original workshop both Mark and Jeff have been extremely successful in getting people development onto the organisation's strategic agenda. This has meant managing upwards and influencing the Directors. SF has been a vital tool for doing this, says Jeff:

'We started off with a strategy full of financial targets. We worked away at the Executive, and managed to get the people factor into the business strategy – albeit as the sixth point out of six. It has since risen to fourth out of seven, and now it sits as first out of seven! Our idea is very strongly that if we have the right organisation in place – the right people with the right skills – then the business results will follow. It's no good striving for growth and change in the business, only to find that as you move forwards you don't have engaged and high calibre people to actually do the work and please our members. We used to have sales targets – now it's turned right over and we've worked out that even products are sold by people!

'The way we work with the rest of the business has changed too. People used to come to tell us what they wanted, we knew it wasn't the right thing, it led to conflict. Now people come along rambling about a problem they have, and we say 'what exactly is it you want?' Often the reply is 'Ummmm – I'm not really sure ....' It gets rid of the confronta-

tion. Sometimes they do know, in which case we take it away and start working on it. Clarity is the thing we come back to again and again – do we know what we want?'

Principles of Positive People Development

We might draw some conclusions from these rich and diverse experiences.

Problem Focused People Development	Solution Focused People Development
What's not happening	What IS happening already
Reducing weaknesses	Building on strengths
Clear ideas about what is wrong	Detailed pictures of what would be better
Large changes are necessary for progress	Well fitting small steps and continuing progress
Learning from what went wrong	Levering from what went right
All learners get the same training	Flexing the learning to fit the learner
Organisational objectives are paramount	Learners' personal objectives also relevant
Trainer must know better than learners	Shared collaboration and creation of knowledge
Training IS the solution	Training is a step on the way to a better future
Growth comes from sales and systems	Growth comes from people

Conclusions

Jeff sums up the experience of Solutions Focus at Chelsea:

'The power of SF is its simplicity. The logic of the approach is obvious, but it's not necessarily intuitive! By following the SF principles to challenge years of inbuilt thinking, you can often find a quick and effective way forward to so many challenges – an essential skill set to develop in people if you want a successful organisation.'

Reference

Ludwig Wittgenstein (1958) Philsophical Investigations (tr. GEM Anscombe) Blackwell

Dr Mark McKergow runs the Centre for Solutions Focus at Work. The Centre develops practical positive approaches to the everyday activity of work – including coaching, evaluation, project management, appraisal, strategic planning and more.

sfwork, 26 Christchurch Road, Cheltenham, GL50 2PL, United Kingdom
+44 8453 707145
www.sfwork.com

Chapter 13

Change is in the eye of the beholder

Improving job satisfaction in Sweden

Co-authors: Björn Johansson and Eva Persson

Organisation: Lund employment office (Arbetsförmedlingen), Sweden

A heavy workload, increased stress at work, rifts in the relationship between staff and management, increased sickness absence. This sounds like a workplace with problems and low morale. The fundamental strengths, competences and commitments that keep the workplace going are not obvious at first glance. But these are the very qualities that provide the foundation and the potential to create a better workplace in the future. In this case, Björn Johansson and Eva Persson from Centre för Lösningfokuserad Utveckling (CLUES) used solution focused coaching to bring hope back to an employment office that had been experiencing difficulties for several years.

In 2000, four small employment offices were merged into one in Lund, in Skåne, the southernmost province of Sweden. Staffan Hållö, an experienced manager who had been in charge of one of the four, took on the role of manager of the new office. About 50 people worked there, advising both employed and unemployed people about rehabilitation, education and work.

Staffan explains: *'There were four different cultures in the office and I wanted to create just one.'* Pointing his hand in a heroic gesture, he continues *'I showed the way and kept a tight rein. This was difficult for many of the staff who were used to making their own decisions and so as time went on, I relaxed my directive style. However, after a couple of years, the employee survey was still showing bad results – there may have been one culture, but they still saw me as a dictator. This really made me think. I thought I had changed my way of leading the office, but if they hadn't noticed, then I hadn't'.*

The action is in the interaction

Ludwig Wittgenstein said 'An 'inner process' is in need of outward criteria.' (Philosophical Investigations 580). SF is part of the post-structural tradition, holding that qualities like leadership are not intrinsic to individuals but emerge as part of the interaction between individuals. All change comes from an observer's point of view; if change is not visible in the world, then there is no change. This is one reason why SF practitioners are so interested in the perceptions of the various participants in a situation.

Ongoing workplace evaluations also showed that there were specific areas where improvements were desirable, including leadership style, the work environment, project and developmental issues, and customers' needs and demands. Staffan knew that it was time to do something about the situation and sought advice from his boss. She wasn't as concerned as Staffan himself – the Lund office wasn't bottom of the heap – but appreciating his desire to do better, she recommended Björn and Eva.

It was important to Staffan that the majority wanted to do something about the situation:

'I asked them if they would agree to involve someone from outside – and they did'.

In the spring of 2005, Björn and Eva were contacted by Staffan and given the task of developing a plan with the staff for a better workplace. They were given a day with all the staff, a half-day follow up six weeks later and another follow up after six months.

They had a further half-day session with the staff a year later after the next annual workplace evaluation. Between these meetings, the staff took responsibility to follow up the work, identifying progress, making adjustments and agreeing on further steps. Björn and Eva made this a condition of their involvement in the work.

Preparations and setting expectations

Björn and Eva wrote to all the employees introducing themselves, inviting them to the workshop and giving details of the plan for the day. They also asked everyone to answer four questions in confidence before the first meeting:

- With regards to the evaluation done six months ago, what is your view of the situation today?
- What do you need to see happen during the day together, to make participating worthwhile for you?
- What do you think your workplace's strengths and qualities are in the face of change?
- Is there anything else you think we should know?

The answers were revealing. Many thought that nothing had changed and some thought that things had got worse – more stress, a bit chaotic, not enough structure. To make the day worthwhile, people wanted an open atmosphere; to listen to each other; to do things they had agreed to do; to look ahead. They saw their strengths as competence, professionalism, pride in their work and humour.

The First Meeting

Coaching 50 people at the same time needs a clear structure from the coaches. Björn and Eva like to keep full group discussions to a minimum and instead give time for reflection, working with clear questions and limited time frames for each activity. They use a wide range of different methods of interacting, reflecting, summarising and developing ideas. They change group formats so that people can work with different colleagues during the day in a variety of constellations. They say that engaging in serious work in this way gives people immediate and visible results of their own contribution:

'When some employees were later asked how they were able to sustain this way of working, one of them answered: 'It was easy to keep the structure of working in small groups, since we have done it before and we know that it is effective.' It showed the importance of not only talking about how to do things, but of doing them together.'

Staffan was keen to be seen as a participant in the day, joining in the exercises like everyone else. Björn and Eva started with an overview of the day, acknowledging that the participants were the experts in their own workplace and that their own role was to help them develop their ideas to create a better workplace. They recognised the tough situation by reading a summary of the e-mailed responses to their questions. The participants were able to reflect, comment and add to the list.

Start by building a firm platform

Time spent building a platform is usually time spent well. Björn and Eva do this in the pre-meeting invitation and in the way they start the day. They acknowledge the difficulties, show respect for the participants' own knowledge and expertise and give compliments for the strengths and qualities.

The participants were invited to set up norms for how they should behave during the day to make it feel safe, respectful and meaningful. Impressed by how they had described their ability to cope, Björn and Eva explored how they had been able to carry on in spite of their difficulties. In smaller groups, participants described the strengths, qualities and approaches that had been helpful and sometimes vital in coping. This is another part of platform building and as Eva points out:

> 'This kind of activity encourages engagement and participation and focuses on participants' own abilities as well as their responsibility to make things go well.'

In order to clarify their personal goals for the project, the participants continued to work in groups of three asking each other the following questions:

- Of all the things you do at work, what are you most pleased with?
- What else?
- So in view of that, and everything else you do, what are you most interested to develop, within the frame of creating a better workplace?

- What will be the first sign telling you that you have come one tiny step forward?

Everyone was then instructed to show appreciation and give compliments for what they heard their colleagues say in this exercise.

Who are 'customers for change'?

This is still part of the platform building – engaging everyone as a 'customer for change'. In SF terms, a 'customer for change' is someone who thinks change is desirable AND is prepared to do something about it. This second component of customer-hood is important: often people recognise that change is needed, but think that it's not their responsibility or not in their spheres of influence to effect the changes. By helping the participants to answer the question 'what's in this for me?', Björn and Eva enhance their motivation and energy.

Looking back to this part of the first session, Lil – who works at the Lund office – says

'I didn't feel very good when I arrived at the meeting, but Björn and Eva asked what we do at work that's good and it was great to see such a long list. Since we have learned about the methods they use, we spend more time finding what works and doing more of it instead of looking at the problem and its whole history. We tell each other what's going well!'

The future perspective – stage one

There were two parts to the work: building a future scenario for a better workplace, with associated projects, and concrete action plans. The first was designed to give a clear and detailed picture of the future visualised along a WWYSH-line (What Would You See Happen). The detail was fleshed out by listing what they already knew about what was going to happen (facts, meetings, activities etc) and then by exploring what progress they would like to be able to report along the way, what they would see developing and growing over the period.

'Imagine it is six months from now ... and that during this period, things here have developed surprisingly well ... You find yourself right

in the middle of things happening as a result of progress and improvements. It's not perfect yet, but as far as you are concerned, .. things are going surprisingly well ... How do you know ... ? What are the signs telling you things have changed? What are you and your colleagues doing differently now? How do your customers know ... ?'

Björn explains

'Our intention with this kind of future oriented question is to expand the frame of reference set by current resources and conditions. It provides a very rich picture, full of nuances, which is realistic but also positively surprising.'

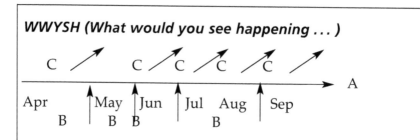

WWYSH (What would you see happening ...)

A shows what 'a better workplace' looks like; B captures known future counters; C represents signs of progress along the way.

During this stage, eight relevant projects were generated. They included how the internal work should be done, interaction between different units, use of competence profiles, how to run effective meetings, activities with customers and the organisation of certain units. Everyone, including Staffan, said which project they thought they best could contribute to, leading to the establishment of new project teams.

Choosing to join working groups gave people the opportunity to work with different colleagues from different parts of the organisation. Lil says

'We worked with different people than we usually did. I had not worked with these people before and after a couple of hours we really worked together. Then I was able to see the problems from another perspective than just my own'

> ### Trust people to choose the most important topics
>
> Offering choice like this is a good way to maintain 'customership' and helps sustain engagement and ownership. Whether people chose a project because it strikes them as most important, most interesting, where they can best make a contribution, or for any other reason, their motivation and involvement is likely to be much higher than if they had been told which project group to join.

The future perspective – stage two

Björn and Eva have devised a Multiple Organisational Projects (MOP) scale process for use in cases like this, where many projects form part of the progress towards the Future Perfect (see box below).

Each project team worked with a scale where 10 meant that their project had developed as well as it possibly could in the next three months and 0 meant that nothing had happened at all. They were asked:

- Imagine you are at 10. How do you know? What are you doing differently? What else?
- Where would you say you are today? (x)
- Of the things that happen at 10, what do you do already, getting you to x?
- Which of the things you are doing already can you do more of to bring you up on the scale?

Björn and Eva's experience is that up to ten project teams can be coached in parallel, making for efficient and effective working with large groups. When each team had worked through the questions about their own scale, the whole group was brought back together for the final steps in this stage:

- Reflection and anchoring where each team reported on their ideas and answered any questions. Other teams were invited to comment and add their views.
- A concrete action plan for the following two weeks.
- Is this enough? If not, what else is needed?

By the end of the day, the eight different teams had worked out concrete action plans, primarily directed towards what they would do over the next couple of weeks. Most of the participants had some action to do within their project team. Björn and Eva gave them only two instructions before they left: to notice when things that they wanted to see more of actually happened and to take small steps in the right direction rather than tackling more than they were sure they could cope with.

Notice what's better and build on it

Once again, we see Björn and Eva trusting the people to get on with things themselves and leaving responsibility for making progress – and noticing it – where it belongs. Notice that their instructions were not 'Make sure you all do your actions' but 'Notice what's better and build on that'.

Björn and Eva discuss the MOP scale process

We have found it very useful to work in two stages when working with larger groups. In the first stage, projects are identified using the WWYSH line. In the second stage, self-selected groups work on the project where they are best able to contribute.

Figure 1: WWYSH

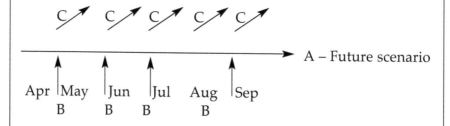

Note: A shows what 'a better workplace' looks like; B captures known future counters; C represents signs of progress along the way.

Every example of progress (C in Fig 1) is directly connected to the overarching future scenario of what a better workplace will look like (A in Fig 1). From the outset, the project is based in context, looking at what is wanted, not what isn't. Useful things which are already known about are acknowledged. These are counters from the future – known contributors to the effective implementation of ideas and plans. Our experience is that this approach creates momentum and security for the employees, without the need to formulate traditional goals or stepping stones to goals.

Projects generated in the first stage are dealt with thoroughly in the second stage, each with a more appropriate and detailed future scenario. This leads to questions about what they are already doing that is useful (how they got to X on the scale in fig 2) and what they can do to build upon that to lead to more progress (X + 1 on the scale). We have found that in approximately 80–90% of these cases, it is enough just to do more of what is already being done.

Figure 2:

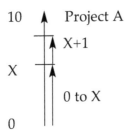

Coaching in parallel sessions is efficient and effective. Each part of the process is given clear time limits and explicit instructions to keep things on track.

The reflection phase involving the whole group can be an interactive and creative period where each group gets feedback, questions can be raised and ideas developed. This part also gives the people interested in several projects the chance to contribute valuable views.

Six weeks follow up

Björn and Eva think that follow up meetings are a less well-developed part of SF working and one that merits more attention. They say:

'This is when some of the crucial qualities for sustainability and continued positive development are found. There is always a range of parallel processes and activities emerging from what has happened and these are often impossible to foresee. The solutions focused approach, asking questions like 'What is better?' allows us to follow up unforeseen improvements and events as well as planned steps, revealing more useful information than simply going through an action plan to check if actions have been done as promised.'

When they met the Lund group again six weeks after the first session, they were primarily interested in what progress had been made, what the participants had done differently and what behaviours they had done more or less of. This gave a base from which to see what further steps might look like, how sustainability could be secured and what new issues might affect the forthcoming work. The follow up meeting was an opportunity to make adjustments to existing projects if necessary. Open questions like 'what is better?' drew attention to unforeseen events, actions and effects developed though out the process. Björn and Eva call this 'emerged progress'.

Remember that Staffan had been concerned at the very beginning of the project about how he was perceived as a leader ('I thought I had changed my way of leading the office, but if they did not think so, then I hadn't'.) Interestingly, several employees reported that they had noticed how the style of leadership had changed in many ways. This happened even though there was no specific action plan about what Staffan should do differently. The clearest connection to leadership was the agreement to change routines at workplace meetings, but this focused on the routines themselves rather than the manager's role. Several employees expressed their astonishment over this effect.

Look out for the 'ripple effect'

Here we see that the question of leadership style is resolved, but it happens indirectly, as part of a whole host of changes in the workplace which emerged over the period. The 'ripple effect' cannot be designed or predicted – but the question 'what's better?' helps us notice it and gives even more to build on.

Participants identified 39 examples of progress and times when things were better. For example:

- Colleagues show an interest and ask questions
- People talk to each other more and exchange information
- Meetings are better prepared. The teams prepare the agenda and send it out in advance
- Meetings are more systematic; there is a chairman and small group discussions
- People participate throughout
- People are more visible to each other and give more feedback and affirmation
- Working with small steps has been different
- People are more relaxed at work, do one thing at a time and get more done
- There's more laughter;
- We talk to each other more

In summary, they reported better routines for meetings and workplace issues, more initiatives from employees, optimism, pleasure in work, better service to customers and increased results. They had discovered that working in a variety of small group settings worked well for them. They had continued to use this approach, letting people choose their projects, with the dual benefits of using motivation, experience and competence to the full and increasing ineractions between colleagues.

Staffan was really pleased by the results and says:

'I had heard of the Solutions Focus approach before, but I work in a very hierarchical organisation and I couldn't see how to introduce it to my small part of it. But what I learned from Björn and Eva is the importance of small steps – you can't do everything at once and you have to start somewhere. The frame we work in may not be negotiable but what happens inside the frame is. We have changed the way we communicate – we used to get everyone together at the same time and the most angry shouted the loudest! Now we ask people to discuss things in small groups for 10 minutes before summarising what they talked about for the larger group.'

Another member of the group, Ann Louise, comments that

'Working in small teams within the big group gives everyone a voice. We listen to each other better and try to understand each other. This gives

the place a family spirit: we're nicer and friendlier and know that we can face the tough times.'

Six months follow up

When Björn and Eva went back to the Lund office six months later, things were going well. There were several small working groups, tackling projects which they themselves had identified and chosen – for example, bullying and sexual harassment in the workplace. Staffan comments:

'The 'ah-ha' for everyone was that small steps get you there: for each project we agreed the target and the first step, but not the rest of the journey.'

Lil agrees. She says:

'Focusing on small steps and not the whole job makes things much easier. We take pleasure in our work and laugh more than we used to.'

Her colleague Stig explains how they decided when a group's work was done:

'We present our findings to the whole office. They listen, make suggestions and decide if anything is missing or if the project is finished. New constellations were composed . . . . like circles in the water. The methods Björn and Eva showed us have given us confidence in our own ability to deal with problems.'

Results

Six months after the first workshop, perceptions of Staffan's leadership style were very different, even though there were no specific action plans focusing on how he should behave. The power of affirmation and appreciation may be relevant here. Asked about times when something unexpected but useful had happened, Ann Louise recalled such an occasion:

'I remember a time when we said good things to Staffan. We could see that it was very important to him and that he was very moved – and he reciprocated!'

As well as a better work environment, the Lund office now had better results. About a year after Björn and Eva first met them, a new workplace evaluation was carried out. It showed an impressive change with improvement in every measured area. In the first diagram the solid line shows Lund office in comparison with the average for their region (dotted line) against a number of criteria. The second diagram shows the situation a year later, after the work with Björn and Eva.

These are impressive results – against every parameter, the Lund office had improved its performance, pulling itself up from well below average to at or very near average in each case.

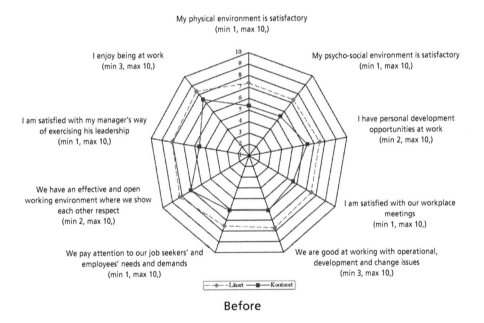

Before

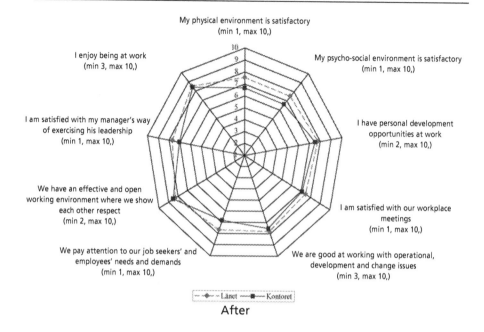

After

Björn and Eva point to three elements of this work as major contributors to its success:

Platform building

'The invitation to everyone to express their views in confidence before-hand enabled us to start the first meeting with a summary built on their own words and descriptions. This let us show that we have recognised and listened to their views. We have learnt over the years that this gives us credibility and saves time talking about how bad the situation is.'

The importance of follow-ups

'The internal follow ups were a powerful learning forum which built participation, efficiency and a platform for decision making. Whether they were discussing improvements or examples of 'counters', both seemed to be helpful learning tools in developing their ideas of how to proceed with each topic.'

Focusing on what's wanted

'If you start by trying to solve problems, you are already trapped in a limited field of possibilities. A wider frame like 'a better workplace' expands this field, is more inviting to participants and is hard to resist.

This gives the group a common project. Individual goals and interests – 'what's in it for me? – are addressed and engaged very early on in the project as part of the platform building process before the first meeting.'

Björn Johansson and Eva Persson are coaches and trainers who have been running CLUES – the Center för lösningsfokuserad utveckling – since 2000. They have been in the frontline of developing SF work in organisations for several years.

Lösningsfokuserad Utveckling, Box 4034, 650 04 Karlstad, Sweden

Björn Johansson bjorn@solutionwork.com
Eva Persson eva@solutionwork.com
www.solutionwork.com/LU/

Chapter 14

Project management – Surprisingly light and successful

How to stage an international conference – without an action plan in sight

Co-authors: The SOLWorld 2007 Interlaken team: Peter Szabó, Daniel Meier, Kirsten Dierolf, Katalin Hankovszky, Urs Limacher Koechlin, Stephanie von Bidder, Felix Hirschburger, Dorothea Schneuwly, Romi Staub, Christoph Ziegler

The SOLWorld conference in Interlaken was a major event with 150 participants and a budget of €95,000. It was staged by an organising team who found themselves engaged in a novel and effective form of project management, which offers new ideas and possibilities for the future.

SOLWorld is an unusual – perhaps unique – 'organisation'. It has no members, no bank account, no officers (president, secretary, treasurer etc). And yet six international conferences and three 'summer universities' have so far been held under its banner, attracting participants from all over the world. It has a website and flourishing listserv. It has nurtured alliances and projects amongst people from different countries and fostered many lasting friendships.

Although there is no committee, there is a Steering Group. The role of Steering Group members includes involvement in building the profile of SOLWorld; adding their names and reputation to SOLWorld events and involvement in the policy development, planning and quality management of future events. Anyone who wants to be on the Steering Group can be on it.

SOLWorld events are organised by individuals or groups. The organisers decide on the event they want to run, and then run it to the best of their ability, drawing on the experience of the other Steering Group members. Anyone can put on a SOLWorld event as long as it has the support of the Steering Group. The organisers risk their own money in hosting the event, and can decide what to do with any profit – including keeping it or passing on, perhaps to support bursaries for participants from developing countries or other good works. This is at the discretion of the organisers who earned the money in the first place.

The 2005 conference was held in Interlaken, Switzerland. It lasted for 3 days. There were 150 participants from 15 countries, 3 plenary sessions and 5 parallel tracks, offering a choice of 5 workshops and live coaching sessions. It cost €95,000 to stage. This is the story of how it was organised, and the lessons for SF project management.

Deciding to do it

Some months before the 2004 conference in Stockholm, Peter Szabó of SolutionSurfers invited a few friends and colleagues on a boat trip in Lucerne. His mission – to discuss with them the idea of hosting the 2005 SOLWorld conference. He had found an ideal venue – the Hotel Beau Rivage in Interlaken – and the hotel was available in May. And it was affordable: May in Switzerland is 'between seasons' – the ski season is over and summer hasn't yet arrived. The friends agreed and the boat trip set the scene for the way the group would work together over the next eighteen months or so – with fun and comradeship. By March 2004, others had joined the group and they all got together in Olten to plan how to introduce themselves as the next hosts at the Stockholm conference when receiving the SOLWorld candlestick (inspired by the Olympic flame).

At this pre-Stockholm meeting, everyone answered these questions:

- *What would need to happen so that it would be worth your while to be a member of the conference organising committee?*
- *What would the conference be like if it were a dream come true for you?*
- *What are the wildest expectations for the conference from the perspectives of the SOLWorld culture of sharing, the participants and the organising team themselves?*

At this meeting, Urs Limacher Koechlin said that he would like to keep track of the finances – but only if he could do so without everyone getting bored or depressed when the subject arose. The group agreed there and then to applaud wildly every time money was mentioned!

Two pages of minutes were produced afterwards, giving everyone a satisfying feeling that although they were written in a light-hearted way, they were serious enough to show how professional they had been. This turned out to be the main function of the minutes – they formed a checklist of sorts. But they were never referred to in subsequent meetings as a way of checking actions.

Getting to work

In June 2004, the whole team went to the hotel in Interlaken for two days 'wasting some time together'. Kirsten explains how the atmosphere was set up:

> 'When we arrived, we wandered around the hotel, imagining it was **our** conference place. We had lunch, toured the hotel and its facilities, strolled around the town and started to dream about the perfect conference. All sorts of ideas were exchanged as we did this together.'

The first task was for everyone to imagine the conference from the moment that the first participant arrived at the railway station in Interlaken until the time when they all left the hotel after a perfect three days together. This detailed mental walk through a perfect conference from everyone's perspective became a regular feature of the team's meetings. Peter says

> 'We took more than two hours over this at our first meeting, starting by seeing ourselves relaxed in the hotel lobby, with everything ready and nothing left to do, waiting for people to arrive.'

A time line was drawn on a flip chart and a list of things to do started to emerge. Then everyone paired up with someone and went out for a walk, discussing as they walked what aspects of the conference they would like to take care of. Stephanie and Kati had the wonderful idea of taking care of 'the stuff that isn't necessary but makes all the difference.' Participants have them to thank for little things that did indeed make all the difference – like the bedtime story placed on everyone's pillow at night. The idea of a 'Treasure chest' emerged – a notional container for great ideas.

A team member recalls

'Looking at the long list of other things to be covered we originally decided to limit our future beam fantasies to 1 hour. But somehow the more we got into it, the more we enjoyed the high level of enthusiasm and energy while everybody contributed thoughts and ideas fertilised by the ideas and thoughts of others. Contrasting ideas were not discussed, just left side by side. Soon we all started to take notes about certain ideas. Somehow there seemed to be this silent common agreement, that what we did was the right thing to do, and that it was OK to go beyond the planned hour. By the time we mentally arrived at the finale – balloons flying off into the skies on the third day – about two and a half hours had passed in no time. And most miraculously all burning questions about pending topics had somehow turned into helpful answers.'

By the end of these two days, the team already had established a working culture in which people felt comfortable and able to say anything.

Peter explains:

'No-one held each other accountable; everyone felt responsible. We felt supported and appreciated in our contribution.'

Taking care is different from being responsible

Asking people what they'd 'like to take care of' has a very different effect and resonance from 'You be responsible for this' or even 'What are you going to be responsible for?'

There were three meetings after this, each lasting a day, supplemented with e-mails and phone conversations from time to time. The team knew how many participants they needed to meet the costs of the venue and had a 'go/no go' date in mind. Each time they met, the 'agenda' (if one can use such a fancy word!) was to go through the event over and over again, asking about the Future Perfect from the perspective of the participants, the programme of events, the Treasure chest and the finances.

Peter is very clear about the value of revisiting the Future Perfect. He quotes Antoine de Saint-Exupéry:

'If you want to build a ship, don't herd people together to collect wood and don't assign them tasks and work, but rather teach them to long for the endless immensity of the sea.'

Although details of the Future Perfect were added and dropped, the feeling it gave the team was very stable.

Felix, who was taking care of the admin, produced a huge to-do list and sent it to everyone, leaving them feeling overwhelmed. At an early teleconference, someone asked Felix if he would be very unhappy if they didn't discuss the list – and he said no – it was enough for him to have tabled it!

Whenever there were differences of opinion about something, the assumption was that whoever was disagreeing must have a very good reason and that the others should be interested in this. They worked hard to achieve a common goal, with these kinds of conversation:

A: I think we should do this.

B: Suppose that happened, how would it be useful?

Or

A: I don't like that idea.

B: What would it have to look like to make it comfortable for you?'

At one stage, with about three months to go, Peter himself was feeling a bit flat. One of the team asked him his position on a happiness scale and asked what one point higher would look like. This is when the idea of including a live coaching track came up.

Scaling – an unreasonably effective tool

Another example of what a simple scaling question can lead to. No wonder we call it an unreasonably effective tool! Simply thinking about a point higher on the scale, rather than some vague idea of 'it should be better', seems to make challenges more concrete and tractable.

A potentially sticky moment came with about four weeks to go to the conference. Kirsten says:

> 'When we had our last meeting before the conference, I was terrified that someone would raise the to-do list. Luckily, someone asked 'What needs to happen today to let you feel comfortable that the conference will go well?' Then we walked through a Future Perfect conference again – much better than tackling a to-do list. People took their own notes during the meeting and said 'I'll do this' when they felt so moved.'

Some things didn't get done, but it didn't matter.

Use the noble art of leaving things undone

The quotation from the Taoist scholar Dr Lin Yutang is relevant here. He says 'Besides the noble art of getting things done, there is the noble art of leaving things undone.' If nobody thinks something is important enough to do, then it probably isn't.

Reflections on what worked

Organising the conference was a highly satisfactory and rewarding process for all the members of the organising team. Never before had any of them experienced a similar lightness and ease in being part of a group doing a complex job.

They have made two deliberate attempts of understanding what made a positive difference a little better:

- During the conference Insoo Kim Berg conducted a one hour interview with the entire team exploring some of the milestones and underlying principles.
- they met for a 2 day retreat 8 months after the conference to reflect on what had worked and what useful stories they could tell about how it worked.

Their findings are still tentative and they are too modest to offer a recipe for solutions focused project management.

> 'Currently one of our most popular explanations is that we were just very lucky. And a large part of our luck was the perfect fit and mix of the team members.'

> ### *Be lucky by expecting to be lucky*
>
> In his book The Luck Factor, Richard Wiseman observes that 'Lucky people expect their interactions with others to be lucky and successful.' This is a combination of knowing what a lucky result would look like, and then noticing when it happens.

In addition to luck, the Interlaken team has identified four helpful principles, which frequently reappeared in their favourite stories about their unique and generatively creative way of managing the project:

- freedom and trust
- the paradox of leadership
- appreciation as a work principle
- confidence and curiosity in difficult situations

Freedom and trust

Team members encouraged each other to develop, to follow their own ideas and act as project leader for their own part of the project. Nobody acted in response to a request or orders, but out of the conviction that everybody would determine his or her own responsibility. This took a lot of trust of all members of the team in the other members' identification with the project and their ability to manage their chosen tasks competently. This combination of freedom and trust meant that it was all right when somebody did not contribute in a meeting, came late or chose to go for a walk instead of joining the meeting. It was assumed that those who were present were exactly the right people to discuss the topic or to do what needed to be done.

'Interestingly enough, a binding agenda did not exist. Detailed lists appeared and were updated and revised. But somehow the team members trusted that everything had to be in flow and that the lists were only a picture of what could be accomplished by the team members because they wanted to tackle it or felt responsible for it.'

'We always had the most important things in place. There was always someone who took notes when important things were discussed in the meetings (at least in the beginning), someone who had the financial situ-

ation in mind, someone who checked essentials with the hotel, etc. But it wasn't planned per se, we did the things we wanted to do and trusted each other that it is exactly the right person in the right time. We trusted each other because we knew that the reason for doing something always came from the wish to organise the conference we dreamed of since our first meeting and not because of achieving some kind of hidden agendas – what a difference!'

'I can remember my conscious decision: just sit there, and that's already good. It is OK if you don't do anything if nothing is there to be done. Just pay attention, then if something turns out to be your job, you go ahead and do it.'

The paradox of leadership

There was never a designated project leader for the work. Peter Szabó had fixed certain critical points before it started (reserving the hotel, inviting certain speakers) and Daniel Meier was responsible for facilitating the team meetings – but nobody carried out classic leadership tasks. It appeared that leadership multiplies when it is divided. Hierarchy is important in rigid structures. There, it serves as a point of orientation and way of clarifying responsibilities. In contrast, the Interlaken team worked in a self-regulating system, constantly evolving and forming a fluid organism which could react very quickly to new influences. This works, if leadership is not centralised but distributed. Thus, in Interlaken everyone took up his or her leadership tasks and responsibilities were taken on in a very fluid and flexible way.

'What was most amazing for me was the insight that I, who had spent years organising and managing at the forefront of management, now found the greatest satisfaction in acting as a helpful 'court jester' in the background asking useful questions for reflection based on my years of experience which supported the people working at the front to achieve top performance.'

'I joined the organising team for SOL 2005 later than some of the others. At my first meeting with them in Basel, nobody could explain to me which function they were fulfilling or which tasks individual team members were dealing with. I was amazed at the fact that they were already able to present such impressive results even though they were working in a free and unstructured way.'

'I often felt responsible for planning and moderating the meetings of the project team – and it has never been so easy for me. Already in our first meeting I was full of trust in the competences and the motivation of the team members. I only prepared two initial questions:

a) What has to happen in this meeting so that it was worth your while coming here?

b) Future Perfect: Imagine this will be an incredibly successful conference: What would happen at the conference?

So I did take up leadership but only to let it go immediately with my questions.'

'Every one of us had a 360° radius of attention and would have been willing and prepared to jump in whenever help or additional work was needed.'

Appreciation as a work principle

In classic project teams, it is often assumed that the project leader should show his or her appreciation to the team members for their work. Since there was no project leader, it was the whole team's shared task to do this – and they did so consistently, by always showing appreciation for what people had done. This might be a short 'thank you' in an email for completing something or a compliment during the meeting. What they were especially good at was appreciative gossip about one another. Whenever they talked about somebody who wasn't in the room at the time, it was about how useful something someone had done, or said or contributed had been.

'A colleague gave me a wonderful compliment about something very small that I had done. I grew at least 3 inches ... and really felt like passing on other compliments!'

'Getting appreciation and trust from people you admire is probably one of the best things you can earn and it results in motivation and willingness to walk the extra mile.'

'The big difference in this team, the 'spirit' was characterised by mutual respect, appreciation and care in interacting with each other. Additionally, the mutual compliments increased motivation continually.'

Confidence and curiosity

Despite all this, there were at times different opinions and ideas in the team. Heated discussions, however, were very rare and they even helped each other to articulate their diverging opinions. Usually, they interpreted such remarks, concerns and different ideas as useful information for reaching the goal. Instead of finding counter arguments, they concentrated on exploring each others' ideas

Solution Focused enquiry helps to continue thinking together instead of trying to push through individual opinions and ideas.

> 'I think the fact that we accepted what each of us needed, that we asked and enquired about what would make it enjoyable for every one, was a key factor in the lightness and warmth of the conference that also spread to the participants.'

> 'What thrills me the most is the result of all the attempts to find a reason or explanation for all of these almost paradoxical incidents. Apparently there is a way of knowing that is completely different. You do know but you don't know what is going on.'

> 'Working on these topics with eight people can be difficult – different ideas emerge, concerns and counter arguments are discussed. In these phases, we always had someone in our group who managed to lean back and ask three questions:

> and what exactly is your goal?

> and how would this idea be useful for our conference?

> and what would a participant say he or she would appreciate in this?

> We wanted to appreciate every statement and develop together, how it could prove useful for our common goal. And that worked.'

Build motivation and organisation with the Future Perfect

This is an excellent example of the power of the Future Perfect tool, especially in its focus on concrete detail and observable features from different perspectives. We think this case has a lot to say about future work practices, as the command and control workplace withers away and self-motivated, self-organised teams become more common.

You can see pictures and materials from the SOLWorld 2005 conference on the SOLWorld website at www.solworld.org.

Reference:
Richard Wiseman (2004), The Luck Factor, London: Arrow Books

Chapter 15

What went well?

Addressing a business disaster with Solutions Focus

Co-author: Dr Hans Zeinhofer MMC

Organisation: Energie AG Vertrieb GmbH

Hans Zeinhofer is the Managing Director of Energie AG Vertrieb GmbH, the sales company within the Energie AG group based at Linz, Upper Austria. He was formerly the Managing Director of Energie Allianz Austria GmbH, Vienna. The company has nearly 100 employees, producing a total turnover of €320 million per annum. It provides electricity and energy services to 425,000 customers in Upper Austria.

Hans took part in the Masters degree course in SF Management with Günter Lueger at the PEF University in Vienna. At the SOL 2006 conference, he related the ways in which he has used SF ideas in his role as a business leader. He says:

The SF tools I work with are simple, but they are also very substantial in practice. I am continually struck by how much these tools can transform difficult situations, and also by how much of a struggle I find it to remember them in practice!

Lessons for leaders

Firstly, I have learned to listen – to really listen – and not come to premature conclusions.

Secondly, I have learned to ask questions – real questions – not statements dressed up in the grammatical shape of questions.

Thirdly, I have learned to see and respect my employees as experts on the problems they are facing – as opposed to seeing myself as the expert who has to sort it out. This has been a great emotional relief for me. A lot of pressure has been lifted from my shoulders since I started to do this.

Fourthly, I have learned to show appreciation, in real and small ways. In trying to incorporate it into my basic attitude I have found that to show appreciation so that people really feel it may not use many words. I find that remembering that employees have the right to be appreciated helps me with this.

Finally, I have learned that the approach I take influences the results I get. A problem focused approach gets totally different results to a solutions focused approach. I have tried to do things in many different ways through my career, and the solutions focused way is best.

A major disaster ... addressed with Solutions Focus

Three years after the complete liberalisation of the electricity market in Austria the wholesale market prices started to climb steeply. As a result the electricity sales companies had to increase their prices. The impact on domestic customers was limited on this occasion, as the grid tariffs were lowered by the regulatory authorities.

The main problem we faced was not the task of communicating a moderate rise in prices but how to do it, without violating our legal obligations. In Austria, the law states that if a consumer does not accept such a price increase and sends a written rejection to the company, the contract automatically ends one month later. The companies are obliged to inform their customers 'in a clear and understandable way' about the consequences of submitting a rejection. If the customer has not found a new supplier after a month, they will be disconnected from the grid.

It was in this communication that the disaster began. The obligatory letter to the customers was written by the legal department. From a legal perspective it was definitely correct, but it gave the wrong impression to our customers (at least those who read it carefully).

During the first week after the mailing the Customer Care Centre received 20,000 calls about the letter. Many customers were totally confused and worried about 'getting disconnected from the grid after having been a loyal customer for 30 years!!'. Even worse, many calls were not answered; the volume of calls was far greater than the capacity of the call centre. Angry articles and letters to the editor appeared in the newspapers, politicians sought to intervene, and the local consumer organisations were also flooded with complaints. It really turned into a worst case scenario.

The senior management in our holding company demanded an 'urgent and complete report'. The departments involved wanted an urgent meeting 'to discuss the reasons for this incredible disaster'. I decided to hold the meeting two weeks later. My first priority was to get things under control and make sure our customers were treated as well as possible.

The meeting

The participants in the meeting – mainly the heads of departments from the sales company, the call centre and the legal department – arrived. The atmosphere was loaded with tension, everybody holding written statements in their hands and waiting to explode with anger. However, as I stood by the flip chart to take down their comments the question I posed was entirely unexpected.

My question was **'What did we do right, what went well?'**

One of the department heads immediately said, 'Hans, we are here to discuss what went wrong, how such a catastrophe could have happened!'

Of course, my question was a very paradoxical intervention. I insisted on everybody concentrating on it, which was not at all easy. I stuck with it, and gently overlooked every single attempt by the participants to change the subject. One and a half hour later the chart was completed.

'What did we do right, what went well?'

- *Only 4 per cent of the customers contacted the call centre*
- *Only 42 contracts were ended (out of 425,000 existing contracts)*
- *30,000 customers decided to choose our new hydro-product*
- *We did good trouble-shooting during the crisis*
- *We co-operated well during the campaign*
- *Our co-operation with the Chambers of Commerce and Agriculture worked well*
- *The negative media coverage was less intense than expected*
- *We strictly followed the relevant laws and regulations*
- *Our customer service concept proved to be effective*
- *We were undertaking useful self-reflection and self-criticism*
- *We would still reach our commercial goals (increase in earnings of €15 million)*

It might be considered normal that the remark about the commercial

goals only came after one and a half hours brainstorming: but this was the reason we did the whole campaign! So somehow it appeared that the main goal had been overlooked during the rush of day to day work. In my view it took so long to remember it because everybody was fixed on the problems and the negative emotions connected with them.
The second question was

'What will we do better (the next time)?'

It took only half an hour to collect the ideas:

- *Get the call centre involved earlier*
- *Only one letter maximum to each customer*
- *Separate the information about changes in the prices for electricity and grid tariffs*
- *Make letters more understandable for the customers (no more legal people involved in the writing!)*
- *Active communication with the media (press conference, press release)*
- *A broader internal pre-information process*
- *Use our own consumer magazine as an information channel instead of separate letters*
- *More detailed internal goals for the campaign*
- *A better concept for internal information*
- *Set up an 'internal control group' for the content of letters*
- *Better ideas for communicating with consumer organisations*

As the list shows, many constructive and future oriented ideas were suggested. Most of them were indeed applied during the next similar campaign. The meeting ended in an obviously positive mood. The report to the senior management consisted of the two lists above. It was some sort of a paradoxical intervention for the senior management as well – it caused some astonishment, but was accepted with obvious relief.

Be brave and gently persistent

Hans' persistence in sticking with his Solutions Focus is an object lesson. Even in this very difficult situation, looking for what went well provided a fast track to useful improvements and practical steps.

Chapter 16

Solutions Focus Working

This book has featured fourteen different examples of Solutions Focus working. In this final chapter Jenny and Mark discuss the overall lessons learned and impressions gained from examining all these cases together.

J: In trying to sum up the lessons from the contributions in this book I had the same dilemma as the one faced by Peter Röhrig's clients in the Cologne hospital system: how do we draw coherent messages out of what seems on the face of it to be a very disparate group of stories? Indeed we referred in the introduction to the difficulty of generalising when we start with the idea that every case is different. Let's talk instead of "family resemblances".

M: That's a good idea. This is the Wittgenstein concept - that although family members don't all look the same, perhaps there are certain commonalities that appear in some family members but not all. And yet we are in no doubt that they are all members of the same family.

J: There are a few features that I have noticed. Firstly, the power of one. Carey's story of how one man made a big difference in the Co-op. And Mona's story of how an individual manager made a difference without, as I understand it, ever mentioning the phrase Solutions Focus. This is quite counter to the suggestion that many people make - that in order to have effective change it must start from the top or be full scale in some way.

M: Yes – this connects up with the idea of the Interactional View that we've mentioned on various occasions. If organisations are the net result of interactions between people, then anyone can do something different that starts things happening differently. This may be picked up and amplified by those around them – or it may not do anything very much, it may just be damped out. I've always found this a very empowering thought: in real life, change can start at the top, but equally it can start at the middle or the bottom. The ideas that are picked up and used and turn out to be effective can start anywhere.

J: Yes – and often without anyone noticing that a change has been encouraged.

M: Yes – it's the natural way that people in groups work together – you see something useful, you join in with it, you do more of it, you don't see this as a change, it's just life – it's just how things go on.

J: At the very opposite extreme, we saw an organisational restructuring which did start from the top. At Freescale Semiconductor the top management were very much involved. But again we saw the differences really being made by the "what's in it for me?" question which was put to everyone in the workshops so that every individual saw the point.

M: In the Freescale workshops there was a huge benefit not just from drawing people into the conversations about what they wanted and then exploring that in great detail but also from the way that those people subsequently went out and interacted with the rest of the organisation, thinking that perhaps this reorganisation might be a useful idea. There are a lot of benefits to that way of tackling things – encouraging a ripple effect to add momentum to useful change.

J: You spoke about increasing awareness in the rest of the organisation there. I was struck by how very often the pursuit of detail was important in these cases – another family resemblance if you like. That awareness of things getting better is enhanced by specifying in advance the kind of better things that one might be looking for.

M: And this is helped by looking at the details of what's happening when things have been better in the past. The detail holds many of the keys to moving forwards. This exploring of detail is something that we find that people **can** do when they're asked to. It's not an instant response to investigate the detail for many managers – they want to get the principle and then move on. This works well until it doesn't … then it's a different tack to go for the detail and stay with it and examine it and see what happens.

J: Yes – it's an interesting phenomenon about $5000 words in general: we think we understand what they mean. And rarely do we discuss the details of how would we know leadership, team work, whatever… if we saw it in the flesh in this particular case?

M: It's vital in terms of SF practice to link these big ideas to real situations and in a real context. The recipe books that you can buy about how to do, for example, better team working are assuming a description of better team working without inquiring about how it is now and how it might be in this particular situation. In SF we have the idea that every case is different: this really is a different **kind** of approach to the conventional "How To" books on the business book-shelf.

J: Another family resemblance which crops up in nearly all of the cases is the question "what's working already, here, in this context?"

M: Yes. That is such a key part of the SF approach. We see it played out in many different ways. Sometimes you examine what's working by imagining what would be better and then looking for traces of that. And in other cases like the Austrian sportswear shop Magazzin they just simply examined the past – when did it go better? And in detail too: What was around? What was helping? How could we do more of that? How can we build on that? I think that particular case is interesting because it doesn't use a future perspective, and yet it's utterly, completely solutions focused – in a very rigorous way. Sometimes people say this is a very future focused approach. It can come across like that but it doesn't have to be and that's what that case demonstrates.

J: It's future focused in the sense of it's what you want – and in brackets are not getting enough of now.

M: As against what's gone wrong in the past and why it's wrong.

J: I suppose it's future focused rather than now focused but, as you say, that doesn't rule out the past. When someone is stuck, the question arises about who is a 'customer': who wants something to be different and is prepared to do something about it.

M: Yes. The importance for the 'customer for change' is a really crucial one in all these cases. Customership can change and people can be drawn into being customers for something, and exploring that makes a huge difference. If you have a group of people who are willing and up for doing something, it's a very different challenge of change than if you as a manager are trying to make something happen – perhaps you've been told to make something happen – but the people are dead against it!

J: One of the family resemblances I noticed in several of the cases was the offer of choice. If you want people to be engaged, then the element of choice, coupled with the idea of "what's in it for me?", seems to be important.

M: Not pulling people along faster than they want to go. It's like leading an animal. If you pull too hard and try to lead it faster than it wants to go it resists – even if it wants to go in the direction you are pulling!

J: Did you notice any other family resemblances?

M: There are a number of branches of the "family": there's one branch where people are using classic SF tools and principles in very nice ways; there's another branch where people are combining these with different tools. For example, continuous improvement and quality in the Sky TV case. Take a fairly classic business tool like a Fishbone causal analysis, call it a "wishbone" and do an analysis of the thing you want and what brings that about. I think there's going to be a lot of potential in exploring some of those practical tools as we go on.

J: That's interesting. I noticed this "other management tools" category too: there's for example Magazzin looking at ordinary financial statistics for positive differences; there's Chelsea looking at various ways to enhance training; there's dealing with complexity – Bayer, Freescale and Cologne. And there is another popular topic - improved team working or team spirit - which wasn't always part of the stated objective. It wasn't top of the list of wants at Bayer or the Ontario Medical Association or the Interlaken conference team, but it was an important by-product.

M: That came out in the Sky TV case as well. Working in an SF way often goes along with energy, motivation and people moving forward with enthusiasm.

J: It reminded me why I am a bit averse to being asked to do team building events or talking about self esteem, or rapport building. Back to the Interactional View: these emerge in the process of doing something; a team becomes a team in the process of doing something, not necessarily in the process of talking about their morale - although the way that they talk about it might be an element.

M: Another example is confidence. Sometimes what looks like people being confident is a by-product of them tackling something they know how to do and want to do. Trying to help someone "be more confident" may be rather confused. It may be easier to help them do something confidently, to place 'confidence' back in a natural and specific environment.

J: Something we must include although it's not a family resemblance is the suggestion that SF isn't a way of life. In normal life, generalising, leaping to conclusions, doing what you always do can be useful.

M: It's what makes the world go round. It's our ability to do these things – to investigate causes, to use abstract language, to act quickly - that makes us human. It's not that we shouldn't do those things. It's that sometimes they lead us into trouble and then we get stuck and the things we're trying don't work and then is a great time to move into this other way of thinking.

J: Have you ever experienced being in a foreign country and you push on the door which says Pull but you didn't know because it's in Chinese or something?

M: What I like about that example is that as soon as you stop pushing and pull on the door marked Pull, you start to feel a change. The door is with you, not against you. I think that sense of "try a small thing" and get some sort of quick response can be really liberating. It's very different to thinking that we have to organise the whole thing in advance. Go through it one door at a time and see what happens. If it's really difficult, break it down into small pieces. This has been a tactic in change for many years of course, back to Milton Erickson and before, and it's something we do well to remember.

J: And it's hugely prevalent in the cases in this book. If you want to go fast, go slow. One of the lessons that many of the clients themselves drew was to take small steps. They said things like "I was trying to do too much. Small steps made all the difference."

M: I was struck that in a couple of cases, the first reaction of the managers was to be slightly disappointed that they hadn't got further. But this was then replaced by satisfaction in the days and weeks that followed, as they saw things begin to pick up speed, and notice that people were moving forwards in a different and purposeful way. I think that all of these interventions are a step on the way.

J: That's important – a step on the way in the direction given often by a well-defined Future Perfect.

M: And that Future Perfect will change in the end of course and the organisation will change its goals and who knows what will happen. One damn thing after another.

J: "Life as we know it Jim".

M: So SF is not a cure for life being one damn thing after another. It is however a cure for life being the same damn thing over and over when it's the thing you don't want.

J: I have one more observation. With the clients that I have met in person, as opposed to over the phone or by e-mail, I was really struck by their enthusiasm for the process and their consultants. When we visited the Lund employment office, and walked through this big open plan office, the pleasure people had in seeing Björn and Eva was palpable. They were really pleased to see them. It brought back memories of the time they had spent together and it reinforced what they had done. The same with Yvonne and Wolfgang from Cologne: there was a real delight in seeing Peter again and remembering the times that they had had. And this works both ways: the research shows that there's an associated benefit – SF practitioners suffer less burnout, they have no qualms about re-meeting clients because they leave them in a good place.

M: In the same vein, all the organisations in the book have agreed to be named and identified. I think that's very unusual. I've read lots and lots of change management books over the years, usually there's an example of a company, but it's a mythical company. To have all the companies willing to be named and stand up and talk about what they have done and the uses they have found for SF ideas is very encouraging.

All these cases have been examples of the SF family in various ways and I hope that people will enjoy reading all the different ones and seeing the connections we've been talking about – and perhaps some that we haven't mentioned.

J: And I think that looking at it through the 'family resemblance' lens may help people to draw their own conclusions from some of the stories in this book. Every case is different but there may be family resemblances.

And perhaps simplicity is a higher level family resemblance.

M: Yes. One way of looking at SF practice is to see it as a way of simplifying – knowing what to overlook and what not to overlook. This gives it a very distinctive flavour. The overarching principle for me of this approach is its practical and philosophical simplicity. It's a rigorous practice and a very distinctive one.

J: And my note of caution is that simple doesn't equal easy. Our training, our education, our understanding of the world is conditioned by this need to "understand" how we got into this damn mess.

M: Understanding things is often thought to be very valuable.

J: But understanding is a different endeavour – it doesn't tell you what to do.

M: And if you want to find what to do, then becoming an expert in what's working seems to be more relevant than becoming an expert in what you don't want. That's the direct route forwards.

Index of Lessons

80 real life lessons for successful organisational change

Bibliography

Robert Axelrod, Harnessing Complexity, Basic Books 2001

Insoo Kim Berg and Peter Szabó, 'Brief Coaching for Lasting Solutions', Norton 2005 – *detailed exposition of Solutions Focused coaching.*

Louis Cauffman with Kirsten Dierolf, 'The Solution Tango: Seven simple steps to solutions in management', Cyan Books 2006

M. Dalziel, S. DeVoge, K. LeMaire, Organizational Redesign in Journal of Organizational Excellence, Vol. 23, Issue 4, pp. 59–64, Autumn 2004

Evan George, Chris Iveson and Harvey Ratner, 'Problem to Solution: Brief therapy with individuals and families', BT Press 1991

Paul Z Jackson, '58 ½ Ways to Improvise in Training', Crown House Publishing 2003

Paul Z Jackson and Mark McKergow, 'The Solutions Focus: Making coaching and change SIMPLE', Nicholas Brealey Publishing, 2nd revised edition 2007 – *comprehensive introduction with many examples*

James Kennedy, 'Swarm Intelligence', Morgan Kaufman 2001

Günter Lueger and Hans-Peter Korn (eds), 'Solution-Focused Management', Rainer Haupp Verlag 2006 – *large collection of papers from the SOLWorld 2006 conference*

Alasdair J Macdonald, 'Solution-focused Therapy: Theory, Research and Practice, London: Sage Publications 2007 – *great collection of research results and practical experience*

Mark McKergow and Jenny Clarke (eds), 'Positive Approaches to Change: Applications of Solutions Focus and Appreciative Inquiry at Work', Solutions Books, 2005 – *leading SF practitioners apply these ideas to coaching, team remotivation, performance management, strategic planning and other areas*

Mark McKergow and Paul Z Jackson, 'Solutions At Work: An

Introduction to Solutions Focused Consulting, Coaching and Facilitation, Solutions Books 2005 – *audio CD featuring a carefully crafted dialogue between the authors*

Daniel Meier, 'Team Coaching with the SolutionCircle: A Practical Guide to Solutions Focused Team Development', Solutions Books 2005 – *SF ideas applied specifically to working with teams*

Thorana Nelson (ed), 'Education and Training in Solution Focused Brief Therapy', Haworth Press 2006

Gunther Schmidt, 'Liebesaffairen zwischen Problem und Lösung', Carl Auer 2004

Steve de Shazer, 'Keys to solution in brief therapy', Norton 1985

Steve de Shazer, 'Clues: Investigating solution in brief therapy', Norton 1988

Steve de Shazer, 'Words Were Originally Magic', Norton 1994

Richard Wiseman, 'The Luck Factor', Arrow Books 2004

Ludwig Wittgenstein, 'Philsophical Investigations' (tr. GEM Anscombe) Blackwell 1958

The New Wave of Change is in SolutionsBooks!

In the 1960s, the legendary record label Impulse! launched itself with the motto 'The New Wave of Jazz is on Impulse!'. The label became the home of legends like John Coltrane and Charles Mingus, and led the way for a whole movement of new musical forms and talent.

In the same way, we now announce that The New Wave of Change is in SolutionsBooks. We will be promoting the developing movement around Solutions Focus and other positive, minimal change technologies including Narrative and Appreciative Inquiry, which value simplicity and pragmatism over complex models and ill-founded theory.

This New Wave is not a different model for change – it is a different *kind* of approach. We are not interested in finding grand designs. Instead, we seek ways to find the direct routes to progress, to explore the limits of what matters and what can be overlooked, in helping people and organisations move forwards in a complex and fluid world.

Solutions Focus is built on the successful field of Solution Focused Brief Therapy (SFBT) as developed by Steve de Shazer and Insoo Kim Berg at the Brief Family Therapy Center, Milwaukee. Over the past fifteen years SFBT practitioners have discovered the power of finding what works, staying at the surface, careful listening and building on small successes, and bypassing conventional therapeutic tools such as diagnosis, cause analysis, 'talking through' the problem and searching for repressed feelings and thoughts.

This radically simple, skilful and subtle practice is found in randomised controlled studies to give as good or better results than more conventional methods, but in less time and with greater satisfaction from clients. Practitioners report fewer features of burn-out than with other approaches. We seek to continue this movement into the worlds of organisations, businesses and other settings.

Some people have found the ideas presented here to be simplistic – nice and positive, just like PollyAnna. We think this misses the point: simple is *not* simplistic. To be less simple, to take less direct routes involving a priori problem analysis, weakness diagnosis and any of the other myriad potential excursions and pitfalls, is to risk at best expending more resources and time than necessary, and at worst spreading confusion and making any problems significantly worse.

Ludwig Wittgenstein wrote that the aim of philosophy was 'to show the fly the way out of the fly-bottle'. In promoting the New Wave of change, our aim is show how simplicity and clarity can minimise confusion and futile effort. Readers will be able to find their own ways out of the bottle.

Mark McKergow and Jenny Clarke
SolutionsBooks

Also published by SolutionsBooks …

Positive Approaches to Change: Applications of Solutions Focus and Appreciative Inquiry at Work, edited by Mark McKergow and Jenny Clarke
£13.99, ISBN 0-9549749-0-5

This collection of articles from the AMED journal Organisations & People describes international experience of applying the positive power of Solutions Focus and Appreciative Inquiry to strategic planning, coaching, performance management, feedback and much more.

'An exceptional collection of international articles on positive approaches to individual and organisational development... These proven, stimulating ideas can be put to immediate practical use by the reader.'
Terry Gibson, Managing Editor, Organisations & People

'A marvellous ensemble of practical articles continuing the worldwide movement towards an appreciative approach to change.'
Neil Samuels, Senior Consultant, BP

Team Coaching with the SolutionCircle: A Practical Guide to Solutions Focused Team Development by Daniel Meier
£17.99, ISBN 0-9549749-1-3

Applying the positive power of Solutions Focus to working with teams, Daniel Meier shows you how to:

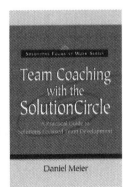

- Apply Solutions Focus methods with groups and teams
- Choose and use the eight steps of the SolutionCircle
- Become an effective team coach – as a manager or external resource
- Engage team members in finding useful action steps
- Use challenges and difficulties in the team to build progress

'Insightful in approach, resourceful in ideas, practical in application, this excellent book meets the needs of both the experienced coach and the manager looking for practical steps.'
Shaun Lincoln, Director of Coaching and Mentoring, Centre for Excellence in Leadership

Order these and other SF books from our online shop at
www.solutionsbooks.com

About sfwork – The Centre for Solutions Focus at Work

sfwork promotes Solutions Focus for leaders from the worlds of work, business, public organisations and beyond. We are developing practical positive  approaches to the everyday activity of work – including coaching, evaluation, project management, appraisal, strategic planning and more.

The Centre is building on experience and practice to develop new ways to do things at work. From leadership philosophies to practical tools, we are using the latest ideas to make things even more simple, and more effective, in the 21st century workplace.

We are part of the development of a 'new psychology', a way of talking about and working with people based on language, discourse and interaction.

sfwork – The Centre for Solution Focus at Work ...

... is a centre for SF in the workplace
... is a centre for people who use SF in their practice
... is a centre exploring the ways SF can help people find what works

Work with us – you will benefit from our years of business experience, wide ranging know-how, best-selling books, brilliant training and consulting skills, and international practitioner community.

Mark McKergow and Jenny Clarke

Co-Directors, sfwork
www.sfwork.com

About the authors

Dr Mark McKergow is an international consultant, speaker and author, as well as a publisher. Many people around the world have been inspired by his work in Solutions Focus - presented wth his inimitable blend of scientific rigour and performance pizazz. He is a global pioneer applying Solutions Focus ideas to organisational and personal change. His book 'The Solutions Focus: the SIMPLE Way to Positive Change' (co-authored with Paul Z Jackson) was published by Nicholas Brealey in 2002 and declared one of the year's top 30 business books in the USA.

A scientist by training and by nature, Mark continues to seek simplicity and reliability in learning and change. His influences range from systems thinking and brain research to language, narrative and philosophy. He has presented on every continent except Antarctica, and is an international conference keynote presenter. Recent clients include Shell, Procter & Gamble, Nationwide, BBDO Canada and Freescale Semiconductor. He was a key figure in starting the SOL conferences in 2002 and is still closely involved with the organisation.

After a career in the energy industry, **Jenny Clarke** has spent the last 15 years as a consultant working as a solutions focused facilitator and trainer, helping people who want to change what they do or how they do it. She works with large organisations who are adapting to change, and as a personal coach to managers and directors. Her strengths are in communication, presentation, consultation and negotiation. Her style is facilitative and enthusiastic.

Jenny has travelled the world hosting workshops for managers, consultants and coaches and has been a regular presenter at the International Alliance for Learning's annual conferences. A founder member of the SOL (Solutions in Organizations Linkup) International Steering Group, Jenny was a key member of the organising committee for the first two SOL international conferences (see www.solworld.org).

Mark and Jenny edited 'Positive Approaches to Change: Applications of Solutions Focus and Appreciative Inquiry at Work', published by SolutionsBooks in 2005.

Index